M000307681

IN THE LURCH

IN THE LURCH

Verbatim Theater and the Crisis of Democratic Deliberation

Ryan Claycomb

University of Michigan Press
Ann Arbor

LIBRARY OF CONGRESS
SURPLUS
DUPLICATE

Copyright © 2023 by Ryan Claycomb
Some rights reserved

CC BY-NC-ND

Note to users: This work is licensed under a Creative Commons Attribution-NonCommercial-NoDerivatives 4.0 International License. A Creative Commons license is only valid when it is applied by the person or entity that holds rights to the licensed work. Works may contain components (e.g., photographs, illustrations, or quotations) to which the rightsholder in the work cannot apply the license. It is ultimately your responsibility to independently evaluate the copyright status of any work or component part of a work you use, in light of your intended use. To view a copy of this license, visit http://creativecommons.org/licenses/by-nc-nd/4.0/

For questions or permissions, please contact um.press.perms@umich.edu

Published in the United States of America by the
University of Michigan Press
Manufactured in the United States of America
Printed on acid-free paper
First published January 2023

A CIP catalog record for this book is available from the British Library.

Library of Congress Cataloging-in-Publication data has been applied for.
ISBN 978-0-472-07574-4 (hardcover : alk. paper)
ISBN 978-0-472-05574-6 (paper : alk. paper)
ISBN 978-0-472-90333-7 (OA)
DOI: https://doi.org/10.3998/mpub.12210885

Contents

Acknowledgments

When a project takes as long to percolate as this one has, it accumulates a long list of people who have offered it love and care along the way. Going all the way back to my first work on Anna Deavere Smith, communities of scholars at University of Maryland, George Washington University, and West Virginia University offered insight that shaped my thinking on this project both directly and indirectly. A decade of working groups at the annual meeting for the American Society for Theatre Research forged several key ideas, particularly James Dennen and Ariel Osterweis's 2011 working group on virtuosity, Sam O'Connell and Ann Folino White's 2013 group on post-truth histories, and Penny Farfan and Lesley Ferris's 2017 group on contemporary feminist playwriting. I am also particularly grateful to colleagues such as Carol Martin, Ariel Watson, and Jenn Stephenson, with whom conversations on theaters of the real continue to inflect my thinking on the subject. Additionally, the writing group led by Andrew Sofer from the 2018 Mellon School of Theater and Performance Research provided timely encouragement, while also asking exactly the right questions for this project to find its eventual shape. At Colorado State University, I owe gratitude to Erin Carignan, the writing partner who helped me get motivated to start writing this project, and to the group of Engaged Humanities Fellows—Kit Hughes, Tori Arthur, Maricela DeMirjyn, Katherine Knobloch, Sarah Payne, and Ken Shockley—who provided invaluable feedback on the book's first real drafts. Thanks also go to the theater-makers whose work strives for a better world: of them, Ping Chong and Company and Porte Parole generously shared manuscripts of not-yet-published material. Of course, I am grateful to the team at University of Michigan Press, especially LeAnn Fields, who never let this project get too far out of mind, and rooted me on all the way through. As a scholar and a friend, Jennifer Kokai gave me the opportunities to think together that rescued this project from oblivion; she gets especial and overdue thanks. And I would be remiss if I did not thank those friends who have invited me to, and joined me in, the theater: Jennifer Ambrosino and Ann Mezger from our days in The Theatre Conspiracy, Kristin Bailey (who invited me to my first performance of *Twilight*), Christy Zink, and Sue Mendelsohn (who joined me at my last one). And finally, to Ann Claycomb, my best theatergoing companion, who reads every one of these words, and has heard every doubt beneath them, I owe something a great deal more than simply gratitude.

Introduction
IN THE LURCH

"Is 'discussion' really so wonderful? Does 'communication' actually exist? What if I were to deny that it does?"[1] So asked the British political philosopher Raymond Geuss in an online article in *The Point*, written on the occasion of social theorist Jürgen Habermas's 90th birthday in 2018. This was a particularly vicious moment to call into question the life work of a thinker whose major and enduring contribution to contemporary theory is the idea of the public sphere as a space in which social ideas can and must be argued and adjudicated; whose 1962 *The Structural Transformation of the Public Sphere* is central to any thinking about what makes a public; and whose monumental 1981 *Theory of Communicative Action* came out in the same year that Geuss himself introduced Habermas's work to the English-speaking world with *The Idea of a Critical Theory: Habermas and the Frankfurt School.*[2] More skeptical some four decades later, the erstwhile disciple chalks up the value of "discussion" and "communication" to a completely unrealizable ideal of the liberal project, an ideal more prone to abuse by the bad actors of liberal democracy than one in service of equality, diversity, and human rights. In *The Point*, Geuss calls out the public sphere of "freestanding, non-theology-based liberalism" as essentially a fiction of western empires, empires largely in decline in the last half of the 20th century, and propped up by its persistence in the US.[3] "Since the events of 9/11 and the economic crisis of September 2008," Geuss writes, "even this sphere is slowly but surely collapsing in on itself under our very eyes. One can see President Donald Trump as acting on the Nietzschean maxim: 'Give what is falling already a further good kick.'"[4]

• • •

In 1977, while Habermas and Geuss were both theorizing the workings of a robust public sphere, theater scholar Gregory Mason was looking back on the previous wave of documentary theater, a wave composed of primarily German work that took on a primarily tribunal form of courtroom documentary. At that moment, Mason hoped for "an imaginative fusion between the known and the possible"[5] in the future of documentary theater. Mason was looking at a form on the wane, but a form that soon would be transformed. What was around the bend in the history of this form was not *immediately* the shift in theatrical technology that he envisioned (though that would come), but rather a broad shift in both the dominant regime of political economy, and the dramaturgical tactics of documentary theater that would follow.[6] Documentary theater would soon leave the hands of political radicals like Erwin Piscator and Peter Weiss, and be taken up by more broadly liberal forces, arising with the advent of the neoliberal moment and working in the centers of liberalism's lingering in the US, UK, and Canada. More narrowly and formally, this shift also occurred in documentary theater's dramaturgical sourcing of material, moving from document-based approaches to account-based ones, which foregrounded interviews of multiple subjects over the presence of official documentation, which hung around as a kind of guarantor of fact. If the dramaturgy of Piscatorian documentary theater was indeed trafficking in outrage, as some have argued, the new verbatim-based forms of Emily Mann and Anna Deavere Smith from the 1980s were based in different kinds of sentiments.[7] These new performances, based in empathy rather than rage, focused on the affective subjectivities of their subjects as documents worth reading rather than on the "objective" facts and documents of earlier modes.

Of course, that shift—which Gary Fisher Dawson described in his 1999 survey of documentary theater as "a new style of documentary theatre in the mode of *drama-vérité*"—is now well-traveled scholarly territory, with an emerging canon of verbatim plays that includes the work of Mann, Smith, Moisés Kaufman and the Tectonic Theater Project, Ping Chong and Company, Tricycle Theatre, and (depending on how narrowly or broadly we define the field) a host of other plays and devised documentary performances.[8] This account-based canon, though, looks less like the soberly theatricalized consideration of justice of the tribunal plays of the German '60s and more like a dramaturgical construction of idealized liberal democracy, a model of the town hall for democratic deliberation, or to put it another way, the Habermasian public sphere. A democratic dramaturgy, placed in this historical context, looks like a specifically western liberal version of theatricalizing our best political selves. It's a version that, like Geuss, I wonder about: in this moment of what I call the "rightward lurch" of western democracies, is this idealized space of democratic deliberation really so wonderful?

This book asks that question in a particularly pointed and self-reflexive way. In what follows, I will trace out a history of this particular branch of documentary theater: performances that rely on verbatim testimony over official documentation in order to model democratic deliberation. The book will look less at the conversations that have tended to animate conversations around documentary theater—that is, about its claims to veracity and "the real"—and more about what political affects these performances seem to have sought. I want to show how the most successful entries into this form (particularly in the English-speaking western liberal democracies) have advanced a political vision of a utopian democratic public sphere, one that seeks to transform dystopian moments of violence into utopian spaces for inclusive and empathetic democracy. I will also illustrate how the rightward lurch of the past seven years or so have exposed that vision as a particular (and particularly cruel) fantasy, with empathy giving way to suspicion and utopian optimism giving way to a nostalgia for a time when we believed that utopia might be possible. But this is not just a disinterested history of that shift, for throughout I will also reflect on my own participation in that fantasy: on scholarly writing that articulated with breathless hopefulness the potential of the form, and on my own theatrical attendance imbued with a belief that witnessing this idealized public sphere was a viable supplement to actual public participation. And finally, this book contains in side comments and footlights an account of the bumpy path through the two years of its writing, marked by two presidential impeachments, an insurrection, a national reckoning with racism, and a global pandemic. At the heart of all of this is a central question: is verbatim theater in the liberal west any longer sufficient to meet the perils of what feels like the possible end of democracy?

● ● ●

I was ruined by Anna Deavere Smith. It happened at a matinee in the winter of 1997, at Ford's Theatre in Washington, DC, at a performance of *Twilight: Los Angeles, 1992*.[9] Smith was just wrapping up her run of that show, just about to take on a residency at Arena Stage, and the performance was by that time so natural, so unforced, as to seem like the artifice had fallen away like chaff, and what remained was the kernel of truthfulness (like, but not precisely the same as, truth itself).

I had just finished my first semester of graduate school and was working as the literary manager for a small feminist theater company in DC. I knew I loved the theater and I had a sense that it was capable of transformative things, but my interest up until that moment had been in the semiotics of the stage—how theater uses signs to tell stories—not about its politics, rhetorics, or social effects. I only knew about Smith's performances in the abstract when I went to see *Twilight: Los Angeles, 1992*. I hadn't yet found her on any syllabi (though I've since put her on several), and didn't then have a sense of her performance as anything more than consuming my theatrical vegetables.

Yet I have visceral memories of that performance: what my theatergoing companion was wearing, the efficiency of the heating system, my seat (house left, 2/3 of the way back), who else was in the theater that day. And, of course, I remember the performance itself: awe at Smith's actorly virtuosity, careening through portrayals of South Central resident Katie Miller's anger about the rioting of Pep Boys; of the wounded obliviousness of Beverly Hills habitué Elaine Young; of the privileged outrage of police commissioner Stanley K. Sheinbaum; of the knowing profundity of Twilight Bey. Implausibly, I *felt* with each of them. At the end of the production, I stayed at my seat for a few extra minutes as the rest of the audience filed out, actively trying to process what I'd just seen, both the performance and what it meant to have witnessed that performance in the circumstances under which I witnessed it—both the cozy privilege of an established theater, and the historic significance of Ford's Theatre in DC. As we walked out of the building, blinking into the winter sun, my companion and I wondered aloud how the other members of the largely white, wealthy audience would respond to that performance. There was a smugness about my wonder, about how other cages had been rattled, without paying attention to my own cage, and the shaking it had just gotten. We talked about the performance all the way home, and I've been talking about it ever since.

Is it over-determined to single out the profound influence of this single performance? Perhaps, but not inaccurate. The deep impact that February afternoon had on me as a spectator changed the way I think about race and about violence in a way that I usually have the luxury of only having to consider from a remove, and the way I was able to think about theater and its capacity for effecting change. I didn't know then that I was beginning a long-term fascination with, and advocacy for, the transformative potential of documentary theater.

● ● ●

In 2003, I argued for "the radical potential that [staged oral history] offers to present difference in the context of community itself . . . even if the politics of the voices presented are often presented in the guise of balance. The form evokes oppositional discourse in its alternative presentation of truth, while it invokes egalitarianism in its refusal to privilege the voices traditionally empowered. Moreover, the form's rhetorical impulse to revise the past through a discursive shift—capitalized upon by progressive playwrights—suggests that these values are necessary to an activist project."[10]

In my dissertation, I defended the "the possibilities of oral history to enact activist work, using community as a space for feminist education, and modeling that ideology through its formal features."[11]

In 2006, I wrote that this form of "political theatre, even when it confronts us with harsh realities, must give us tools and avenues to change them."[12]

In 2009, I delivered a plenary talk at an oral history conference and argued: "we imagine the impact of theatrical space—the venue of oral history performance—as marked by possibility, as the rehearsal of 'place' for utopia, glimpsed in the here and now of the audience."[13]

I have quoted Della Pollock, *so many times*, saying, "the essential promise of oral history performance: that the body remembering, the bodies remembered, and the bodies listening in order to remember ('you remember, I told you . . .') will be redeemed in some kind of change," that I have memorized the quote.[14] *"Redeemed"!*

In 2012, I published an article critiquing some of these plays, but still saying, "I remain more hopeful about oral history performance. Jill Dolan maintains that the utopian performative offers only glimpses of utopia, rather than utopian spaces themselves.[15] The most appealing promise of oral history performance is its aim to take monologic speech and imaginatively re-frame it as dialogue, modeling that process for audiences who believe dialogue to be the clearest path to remedy political injustice, particularly injustice marked with violence."[16]

In 2013, I presented a paper that said such account-based documentary performance "seeks a very humanistic solace in the redemption found in the connections made by individual human selves."[17]

In summer of 2021, I published an essay first submitted two years earlier about Anna Deavere Smith's *Let Me Down Easy* that argued that the "performance both presents and enacts opportunities for mutuality. That is, even as [Smith] shows the audience people to care about, she also models that care by performing them, and performing the event of having sat with them to listen to their stories."[18]

All of these things I have written and presented are shot through with optimism and hope, and now even when I read them, I do so with a nostalgia for a moment when I believed them. All of them were going to find their way into a book I've been slowly working on for years, a book that, having finally turned to it in earnest, I am not sure I believe anymore. If, as Raymond Geuss writes, "The soft nostalgic breeze of late liberalism that wafts through the writings of Habermas carries along with it the voice of a particular historical epoch," I cannot help but to wonder if he is not also writing too about *Fires in the Mirror*, and *The Laramie Project*, and *Talking to Terrorists*.[19]

For years, I have been writing about the promise of documentary, verbatim, and oral history performance. At some level, I attribute this stance to a fairly thoroughgoing interpellation into a white liberal ideology that links social change with indirect measures like "empathy" and "deliberation," rather than direct action. So in this moment, I approach this material with a somewhat different thesis in mind: that verbatim theater from the neoliberal period is characterized by a shift away from polemical presentation of official documentation to an ostensibly even-handed dramaturgy of democratic deliberation, a formal theatrical rendering of the ideal of the public sphere. But while those pieces—many among the most prominent performances of western theater over this period—are deeply invested in the promise (as Della Pollock says) of change, their methods (rooted in affects of empathy and optimism) are no match for the end of empathy and increased suspicion that has characterized the hard-right tilt of our recent moment. Three recent productions bear this out: Anna Deavere Smith's *Notes from the Field*, which opened off-Broadway in late 2015 in the context of the #Black-

LivesMatter movement and in the run-up to the racially charged election of President Donald Trump; *My Country; A Work in Progress*, a play on the recent Brexit referendum by then-British-poet-laureate Carol Ann Duffy and National Theatre Artistic Director Rufus Norris, produced at the National Theatre in London in January 2017; and Montreal-based company Porte Parole's project *The Assembly*, a multi-city documentary project beginning in late 2017 that, according to the company's website, "has been curating and recording encounters in which four Canadians of wildly different ideological leanings face off and collectively confront the issues that most divide them. . . . The actors play these real-life people whose conversations were recorded, transcribed and then edited to create a script."[20]

• • •

To understand how we got to this moment, it might be useful to survey a short history of recent documentary theater. While the formal history of account-based documentary theater has developed and shifted over the forty years since Gregory Mason looked forward to "an imaginative fusion between the known and the possible," its most prominent entries all seem to land roughly in a left-of-center liberal democratic space, aligning with mainline Democrats in the US, centrist Labour in the UK, and Liberals in Canada. Stage one of this history covers the spectacular epic theater polemics of Erwin Piscator and controversial Living Newspapers of the Federal Theatre Project in the US in the 1930s; the sober tribunal plays of the post-war German '60s, and the work of Joan Littlewood in roughly the same period comprises stage two.[21] The third stage of this form developed in its infancy during the height of the cold war, with early entries in the UK, like Peter Cheeseman's work with the Victoria Theatre, Stoke-on-Trent, and in Canada, like Paul Thompson's *The Farm Show*, marking a shift that, as Alan Filewod notes, "tends to document experience rather than facts."[22] This newer approach, taken up in the US by Mann and Smith, focused on local concerns but decidedly national identities; what does the subtitle of Smith's overarching series title *On the Road: A Search for American Character* indicate if not an engagement in the ideal national liberal subject? This iteration burgeoned in the 1990s with Smith's most prominent performances, the birth of Tectonic Theater, and (should we define broadly enough to include it) Eve Ensler's *The Vagina Monologues*.[23] This post-Berlin-wall moment, the supposed end of history, represents what might be understood as the form's most idealistic expression, an expansion outward of its local focus, and a deep investment in staging a utopian public sphere where democratic deliberation runs on the fuel, not just of good-faith argumentation but also deeply humane empathy.

Of course, the end-of-history illusion burst with the events of September 11, 2001—a moment that Raymond Geuss identifies as the beginning of the end of the western liberal project—and the test of liberal democratic principles embodied in the resulting "War on Terror" saw a new efflorescence of the form. The fourth stage of documentary theater encompasses the stretch from 2004 to 2008 that commentators like playwright David Edgar called "the predominance and resilience of verbatim, witness and testimony theatre" and "the rise of a theatre of reportage rather than enactment."[24] The period includes, in a short burst, Robin Soans's *Talking to Terrorists*, David Hare's *Stuff Happens*, Ping Chong's work with refugee children, the establishment of Tricycle Theatre's documentary practice, and Carol Martin's special issue in *TDR* on documentary theater.[25] As the works that appeared in this period expanded their focus to a national and international scope, we might be less surprised to find that oral history methodologies were brought alongside tribunal ones, as the document and the account really fully shared the stage. Empathy still occupied the heart of many of these plays' affective orientations, but most of them were also staging more pointed protests in the face of what liberals in the western democracies saw as neoconservative injustices, or worse, betrayals of democracy. In the face of such betrayals, these performances asserted the democratic dramaturgies of verbatim performance with a greater fervor, straining their claims to even-handedness in service of more pointedly political theater.

This brief history, then, has found verbatim theater's most recent repurposing in the context of the lurch rightward of several western liberal democracies with the Brexit vote and election of President Donald Trump in 2016: stage five. The range of theatrical events of the last forty years or so that might fall under the umbrella of "the theater of the real" far exceeds the scope of this project, and excellent considerations of the taxonomies of form precede nearly every study.[26] As for me, I focus *mostly* on those plays that purport to tell a true story using dramatic text largely or exclusively drawn from the words of people interviewed for the purpose of staging their words in the plays that audiences see. Some of the plays I am thinking of have more or less text taken from other documentary sources. Some of them incorporate stylized framing or creative interweaving of text from a playwright and/

or director. They do not all adhere to the rigor of professional oral history or ethnographic practices (few do, in truth), but they all seem to be working in good faith to represent the voices of real people discussing events and issues of local, national, and even international import. These last three stages, then, roughly correspond to the recent stages of liberal democracy in the neoliberal period, for which account-based verbatim theater as a distinct dramaturgy within documentary theater has been developed, polished, and resuscitated in the service of a center-left-leaning liberal democratic politics of individual voices within a theatrical *demos*.[27]

● ● ●

There are three threads that run through this project, premises that ask me to consider what work verbatim documentary theater has been trying to do since the late '70s, force me to consider my own political stakes in that project, and demand that I reassess the form and my own interest in it in a political moment that feels—quite suddenly—monumentally altered. The first premise is that these plays seek almost doggedly to stage an idealized public sphere for democratic deliberation. These "democratic dramaturgies" frequently represent a kind of town-hall style form of democratic deliberation: many voices, each granted roughly equal standing to tell presumably true stories that represent their perspective and their position on a matter of import. There is a simple, if significant, act of citizen-subject construction at work in these plays, and that construction is constituted by this theatricalized public sphere, even as those individual voices constitute that sphere itself. In the first part of the project, I'll consider how the work of this form stages this idealized public sphere as a way of presenting a model for democratic deliberation.[28] The examples include the famous ones—Emily Mann's *Greensboro: A Requiem*; Anna Deavere Smith's *Fires in the Mirror: Crown Heights* and *Twilight: Los Angeles, 1992*—plays I consider precisely because their prominence speaks to a public investment in the visions of democracy presented to us as—explicitly—a mirror held up to nature.[29]

The second premise is that the public sphere is a spatial metaphor, and idealized political spaces—utopias—have a long history in the western liberal imagination. I began the earliest stages of this project thinking about utopia in performance at a moment when Jill Dolan's work on utopian performatives was first appearing. But utopias, like public spheres, aren't just fantasies of discourse; they're fantasies of place, and I find it no surprise that many of these performances are built around—even named after—physical locations. Crown Heights and Los Angeles and Greensboro (as above), but also Laramie and Guantánamo—which I will examine more closely in the context of place—and scores of community-centered performances that are never performed beyond the boundaries of the communities they represent: these ersatz utopias form the inquiry of my second section. How, I have often wondered, do we manage to fantasize about idealized public spheres in the shape of some of our dysfunctional if not downright dystopian physical places? What phenomenology of theatrical space allows us to understand sites of hate crimes, riots, and torture as venues to meditate on democratic deliberation? For a long time I have understood this imaginative act as one of great hopefulness, a testament to the theater's power to help us salvage even the most painful sites of our recent historical past. I wonder now if that hopefulness is not also a collective form of political naívеté.

And finally, the third thread is the affective orientation of these utopian public spheres toward empathy. Writing and criticism on verbatim theater is awash in the language of empathy—of listening, of "travel from the self to the other" as Smith puts it. If the democratic deliberation of verbatim theater is predicated on the utopian fantasy of an egalitarian public sphere, then its mechanism is not just rational deliberation, but affective connection as well. Cognitive theorists in rhetoric and literature speak persuasively of the role of empathy in both public deliberation and any figurative imagining of the other;[30] performance theorists and historians alike have pointed out how empathy is both an affective phenomenon and an embodied one.[31] Particularly in discourses of race, where Smith's work as well as that of many others have concentrated, empathy has a long history at the center of reparative discourse. The third section considers a range of performances—including Ping Chong's work with refugee children and people with disabilities—in which empathy is both structurally framed and often directly thematized as the precondition for ethical deliberation: the presumption that we must acknowledge deeply one another's humanity before we can solve any problems that might befall our community, nation, or world.

• • •

These are the ingredients for the liberal fantasy of account-based documentary theater: when we (by which I tend to mean, left-leaning often-white liberals who travel through the theater world) strike upon an issue that requires mature and sustained deliberation, we go out and interview dozens or even hundreds of stakeholders, we assemble their voices into a collage of community that attempts to rebalance imbalances of power, and we build a utopian public sphere on ground where injustice and disfunction usually stands, and there we model and insist upon empathetic listening as a crucial step toward solving our problems.

What is this, if not "the theatre of good intentions" (to borrow Dani Snyder-Young's phrase)?[32] Why is it our go-to model?

● ● ●

If this model functioned for three neoliberal decades, why did it recede soon after that war-on-terror boom? And when it returned in the rightward political lurch of the last part of the last decade, why did it seem to ring hollow for audiences and critics? Another way of asking these questions would be to observe some obvious changes: that during the comfortably liberal era of Barack Obama, Justin Trudeau, and (initially at least) Gordon Brown, theater practitioners felt a less urgent need to stage documentary theater as a response to a perceived crisis in democracy. To be sure, instances of theater of the real continued through this period, but they often took more decidedly political forms, relying on other sorts of documents than the personal account and often tackling more widely global issues rather than issues of western liberal national or local politics.

During this period, a seismic shift: austerity, birthers, the Tea Party, Occupy, the liberatory promise of the Arab Spring yielding only one tenuous democracy and a global refugee crisis, #BlackLivesMatter and the range of angry white reactions, Russian bots on social media, climate change denial, Brexit, the rise of strongmen leaders worldwide, and a newly virulent wave of white supremacy—and then 2020 arrived.[33] In that time, and a long time coming, our suspicion of one another across political, cultural, and racial/ethnic lines has begun to overtake our capacity for something like empathy to lubricate an appropriately functioning public sphere. Suspicion is not just the "mood and method" for literary studies, as Rita Felski has observed—it pervades the sites of nearly every social exchange.[34] I am, of course, speaking in broad generalizations here, but the broadly general lines describe what is happening on the documentary stage as well. That is, suspicion extended beyond political discourse among fellow citizens to documentary theater itself, as Mike Daisey's *The Agony and Ecstasy of Steve Jobs* stirred up an authenticity controversy to rival the one surrounding James Frey's *A Million Little Pieces* in 2006.[35] In light of this moment of suspicion, the fourth part of this project will consider the three recent entries into the form that I mentioned above—*Notes from the Field*, *My Country*, and *The Assembly*—as they reveal the fault lines (already fissuring) in the space of democratic deliberation, the utopian impulse, and the capacity for empathetic listening. They reveal a sense that a theater of the real no longer points the way toward real political progress but toward, as Jenn Stephenson identifies in her book of the same title, insecurity.[36]

I wonder, too, about the return of performances like *The Laramie Project* on the 20th anniversary of Matthew Shepard's death, or the Signature Theatre revivals of *Fires in the Mirror* and *Twilight* with actors other than Smith (the latter postponed by the pandemic shuttering of the theaters). What are we doing as a culture with these productions, now history plays? Does *Laramie* now have more in common with Thornton Wilder's *Our Town* (with which it is sometimes produced in rep)[37] than with, for example, Catalan documentary theater-maker Didier Ruiz's 2018 *TRANS*?[38] Can a revival of *Twilight* after the protests of June 2020 make us feel that we have moved forward in the three decades since the LA "riots" of 1992? Or backwards? In sum, this project is not just about verbatim theater, but about a cultural transformation, and how a change in history has marked a change in the politics of form. It is also a reminder that art doesn't spring forth from a vacuum and that sometimes the ideals and values of one cultural moment can seem quaint, nostalgic, even hopelessly naïve in the context of a more cynical and suspicious moment. Sometimes those moments are separated by almost no time at all.

1 *Democratic Deliberation and the Theatricalized Public Sphere*

"What makes documentary theatre political?" Minou Arjomand bluntly asks in a recent article on Erwin Piscator.[1] In her reading of Piscator's later-career collaborations with German playwright Peter Weiss—what I would argue constitute the quintessential performances of documentary theater's tribunal-focused second stage—Arjomand gets more specific, arguing that the "political intervention of documentary theater is to disseminate information, often information that stirs moral outrage."[2] But I have already argued that in the neoliberal period after Piscator's documentary work, verbatim theater marked a dramaturgical shift in preference for source material from the document to the account, a shift attended by both cultural and political contexts. Clas Zilliacus, writing in 1972, locates the burgeoning of documentary methodologies in Germany in the '60s within its specific cultural moment. "The situation," he writes, "demanded extreme sobriety in language and watchfulness against the semantic dislocations of the Nazi era, and the recent past was heavy with themes that could neither be bypassed nor fictionalized."[3]

Certainly, documentary theater's formal structures nearly always reflect their political investments, even when the performances themselves are not explicitly political. But the political is not always as evident in the work that began to emerge in the '70s and '80s and flourished in the decade or so after. Broadly speaking, the period from about 1991 to 2006 produced much of the richest, best-received, and most high-profile (however we might define and measure that) account-based documentary theater in the form's comparatively brief history, beginning with *Fires in the Mirror: Crown Heights*, and including Tectonic's landmark *The Laramie Project*, Blank and Jensen's *The Exonerated*, Wright's *I am My Own Wife*, Slovo and Brittain's *Guantanamo: 'Honor Bound to Defend Freedom'* and other Tricycle Theatre productions, Soans's *Talking to Terrorists*, the work of Alecky Blythe and Recorded Delivery, and numerous entries in Ping Chong's *Undesirable Elements* series. Such a history should also consider the many smaller community-centered account-based performances that proliferated in the period: too many to count. Yet the political stakes in these plays are not always clear, especially when their politics are representational or locally focused, or their explicit stances on policies or practices may be hidden or downplayed.

While there are few published scripts, revivals, or even reviews to mark them, the group of local community-centered productions tells us the most about the political thread that does run through these performances. And while few of them—whether nationally prominent or community-oriented—take strong and specific political stances, they do share a political orientation: an investment in the idea of the town hall as a space for a community to deliberate on matters of real (read: significant, and also read: nonfictional) import.

What might I say then about the documentary form that emerges in latter-day allied-power, post-Cold-War-era liberal democracies—primarily the US, UK, and Canada? Reframed in this context, verbatim theater begins to look not like a soberly theatricalized consideration of justice, but rather like a dramaturgical construction of idealized liberal democracy. A democratic dramaturgy, placed in this historical context, looks like a specifically western version of theatricalizing our best political selves. Some features of this dramaturgy include:

- An emphasis on representative voices—an expression both of representative democracy and the "one voice, one vote" principle;
- The inclusion of "public opinion" voices that have the effect of bracketing and diluting the emphasis of even the most powerful individual voices;
- An emphasis on even-handedness and the appearance of neutrality, even when a specific stance is comparatively evident;
- A narrative open-endedness and a refusal to draw conclusions—a

theatrical process designed to look more like discussion than prosecution;
- The introduction of affective information—how these crises *feel* to individuals and not just how the rational frameworks of state apparatuses might determine outcomes.

This is hardly an exhaustive list of features of these performances; nonetheless, they point to how theatrical structures have been crafted to come alongside idealized processes of democratic deliberation that have occupied a particular political place in the recent history of theater in these nations.

If this liberal-democratic form of documentary theater might be said to have a documentary theater precursor other than the Piscator line, we would look to the Living Newspaper performances of the Federal Theatre Project in the US in the 1930s. These performances, influenced by Piscator's Marxist work in the '20s and '30s, as well as by early Soviet propaganda, combined documentary theater, spectacular scenography, agit-prop, vaudeville and sentimental narrative to dramatize issues of current concern.[4] While not a wildly successful form of political theater in the era, caught as it was between the leftist sentiments of its creators and a federal funding model that sought to tamp down its most politicized sentiments, the Living Newspapers did introduce into their documentary impulses the "little man" figure. Typically a single figure in the play, this figure posed questions that an audience member might have, or expressed opinions that might be held by the "general public," represented in and by the audience.[5] While this figure hardly represents the full commitment to democratic deliberation of, say, *Twilight: Los Angeles, 1992*, the figure does stand in for both the subject of a representative liberal democracy and of the everyday. The "little"-ness of this figure, along with the formal dramaturgical structure, developed over time into a lineage that Jacob Gallagher-Ross calls "aesthetic democracy."[6]

This is to say that insofar as the "little man" is a distinctive feature of the later Living Newspapers, it also draws early documentary theater into a US context in a way that brings democratic imaginaries into view, by briefly interpellating the everyday citizen into the play's deliberations. Gallagher-Ross locates two particularly American traditions of the ordinary in its theater, the first being the Arthur-Miller-esque tragedy of the common man, a realist aesthetic that depicts ordinary people "struggling against an immutable universe."[7] The second, and the subject of Gallagher-Ross's scrutiny, is something more fleeting, found in "new theatrical forms and aesthetics [that] focus spectators' attention on the perishable or habitually invisible aspects of everyday experience, the material objects that populate it, the evanescent words and thoughts people use to make sensible shapes of reality's unimaginable surfeit."[8] For these artists, he argues, "the everyday becomes a space in which to negotiate the competing demands of innovative form and democratic availability." Aesthetic democracy, then, comes to exist in a reordering of the priorities of the momentous and the quotidian, with the latter offering new perceptual models to artists and spectators alike.

Recent models of this kind of verbatim theater certainly do not dispense with the momentous event, as Gallagher-Ross's subjects do: riots and wars and murders and national alignments are around the corner in these performances, if not directly onstage. Yet these productions are nonetheless interested in the kinds of new forms and perceptual reorientation involved in remaking Realism to meet new democratic demands—attending to quotidian voices who might disappear from local and national discourses, in order to hail new kinds of subjects. Smith, for example, often helps illustrate this continuity between "everyday people" realisms and Gallagher-Ross's aesthetic democracy through the props and costumes that signify her quick character changes. These everyday objects do not disappear from the stage when she moves on to a new character, yet while they are never directly picked back up in performance, Smith regularly gestures to these objects during her curtain call in the way that another star might gesture to her co-stars, reactivating the often-ordinary people for whom these objects metonymically stand.

These (literal) gestures to a formal aesthetic democracy do not place these performances directly within the US avant-garde tradition that Gallagher-Ross describes, but the aesthetic affinities nonetheless underscore the commitments to democratic representation that these performances implicitly (and often explicitly) entail. Recognizing that these performances do not represent a coherent genre, per se, but rather a collection of dramaturgical strategies that choose to source not just the official and the momentous, but also (and often determinedly) the unsanctioned and the ordinary, I would like to show in this cluster of plays an endeavor to make onstage a microcosm of utopian democracy. What emerges from these dramaturgies is a loosely related set of fantasies about how the subject is constructed in western liberal democracy, how liberal discourse hails audiences to participate in this vision of liberal democracy, and how the ideals and perils of this vision are replicated in performance.

If the heart of these performances is the speaking subject, as individual and collective, it seems worthwhile to consider how they tend to construct subjectivity in relation to their conception of democratic deliberation. I understand that while document-based theater *tends* to draw its source material from the trove of documents already in the official sanction, and therefore already part of the ideological superstructure of its culture, the account-based material of verbatim theater is produced and entered into the culture through a series of actions, all of which have the effect of shaping the speaking subject within this staged framework of liberal democracy. Of course, we *value* the speaking subject as the hallmark of representative democratic governance. We speak of "making your voice heard with your vote" and "the voice of the people" when we speak of elections and referenda; peaceful protests are often registered as "speaking truth to power." While these frames of democratic participation also include embodiment and mobility, the consistent use of the voice as metaphor clearly implies the way that speaking subjectivity matters in this structure, and that in the imagination of these performances, coming to voice represents a kind of representational citizenship on the space of the stage. This is a remarkable conflation of subject into citizen made possible in the imaginative space of the theater, one with fewer gates to pass through toward "citizenship." Here, being represented as a voice and (usually) a body onstage is both the privilege and price of participation in this democratic deliberation. But this representational naturalization (as both a process of citizenship and an elision of artifice) is nonetheless shaped by discourse and ideology, by a series of processes less onerous, but no less selective, than national citizenship.

Representational citizenship in the deliberative spaces of verbatim theater, then, entails several familiar processes that bring the speaking subject into line with the ideological structures of the performance. First: the interview itself. While staging the interviewer and the site of the interview exchange is often a utopian act invested, as Della Pollock describes, in the promise of future change, it is also precisely the kind of act of confession that Michel Foucault famously describes as ambivalent act, constituting the speaking subject while making the speaker subject to power.[9] That power may be attenuated in the form of the theater-maker, but it is no less part of an ideological structure, in this case an ideology invested in a form of democratic deliberation. In this way, the interview subject—the speaking subject—is also a subject constructed by ideology, à la Louis Althusser.[10] Representational citizenship in the verbatim theater, then, means becoming a subject of and subject to the theater's ground-rules for representational democracy. The process does not end there, though, because insofar as many of these plays are built upon various configurations of representative diversity in both the form of the actors and the represented subjects, they also "hail" their audiences—*you can empathize with me, identify with me*—to join the shared space of deliberation. This is precisely the process that Althusser calls *interpellation*, and it is the signal process of ideological regimes. There is no outside of it, and given that the theater has always been a polyvocal space of contested ideologies, it is no surprise to find not just the flows of ideology here, but that those ideologies in the kinds of mainstream venues in the US, UK, and Canada that mount these performances would be deeply consistent with the national imaginaries of liberal democratic structures.

At their most idealistic, these are performances predicated upon the inclusion of more voices in more equitable arrangements than are framed elsewhere in the popular imagination, and certainly in the deliberative processes of actual democratic political participation. The goal of these performances seems, fairly universally, to be to grant a wide range of voices privilege to speak by experience or insight, rather than by preexisting empowerment, to deliberate about events and issues of public significance, and to enact positive (often liberal, given the orientation of most theatermakers in these contexts) social and political change. But with that structure of liberal democracy as an organizing principle, these performances often both reflect and respond to the shift in the 1980s through the aughts toward a thoroughgoing neoliberalism. This trend in the theater also corresponds with what some might describe as the deliberative turn in the field of political communication and social theory, a current marked by the work of Seyla Benhabib, Iris Marion Young, Robert Goodin, and others. It will be useful to briefly engage some of this literature throughout, especially as it connects theories of the public sphere from Hannah Arendt and John Dewey to Jürgen Habermas and John Rawls to recent social theory on neoliberalism and culture.

And, of course, while by now it is almost commonplace to attribute social-political-economic echoes in any recent moment to the deleterious effects of neoliberalism, I would suggest that this particular convergence of theatrical form and political history can be attributed precisely to this movement in political economy, and its attendant cultural movement as well. That is to say, this particular theatrical assertion of liberalism is both a response to and a participant in the incursion of neoliberal ideology into the bourgeois liberal project. In tracing out this ideological history, David Harvey identifies neoliberalism as hinging upon "liberating individual entrepreneurial freedoms and skills within an institutional framework characterized by strong private property rights, free markets, and free trade."[11] This logic, Harvey and others note, entails not just prioritizing market logics, but by extension, limiting governmental regulation and prioritizing short-term contractual relations, a set of logics that have wide ranging cultural effect.[12] Along the same lines, Lisa Duggan notes how this aggressive assertion of market logics presses against notions of the public, from higher education through to other forms of knowledge. "Neoliberal campaigns to downsize public education also aimed to largely abolish the public nature of support for broad-based access to knowledge and information," and with this "incredible shrinking public"[13] I read not simply public universities, but more broadly, a well-educated rational public sphere as well. And more recently, Wendy Brown has argued that this phenomenon of economization of *all* public value has undermined "principles of speech, deliberation, law, popular sovereignty, participation, education, public goods, and shared power."[14] If we accept this narrative of an encroaching redefinition of public value and power as a shift *toward* marketplace-driven power and *away from* the public sphere, we can see these plays as seeking to formally enact a remedy to this shift.

And yet, these performances also operate in particular and defining ways *alongside* the political economies of late market capitalism; I might even suggest that the most prominent of these performances are invested in the vantage point of a kind of bourgeois liberalism. While there is much work to be done toward a political economy of "establishment" contemporary theater, one way we can find this vantage point reflected is the infrastructure of well-supported regional theaters and other cultural institutions where these plays often appear. The Mark Taper Forum in LA, Arena Stage in DC, the McCarter Theatre Center in New Jersey, the National Theatre in London, as well as Off-Broadway, West End, and Toronto Theatre District venues, are all regularly host to such verbatim performances, as are many universities, colleges, and other large community cultural centers. Insofar as these venues choose their shows to appeal to not just audiences but also boards of directors, grantmaking entities, and private donors, the ideological range of these performances narrows, and the likely audiences get even narrower. This usually white, middle-class audience is already well-represented in western liberal democratic structures; interpellation into the deliberative spaces of these stages is only ever mildly uncomfortable, certainly when viewed against the disproportionate sense of affirmation that comes from passively witnessing these performances. But in general, these plays' deliberative modes also entail a reluctance to draw conclusions that connect to the risk-averse material circumstances of middlebrow theaters; and the narrow band of audiences implied there creates an asymmetrical construction of any given performance's imagined democracy. The values that get pulled along with this fantasy of democratic deliberation, then, are often the same set of values that are built into the formal institutions of western liberal democracy: if not overt racism, sexism, heterosexism, ableism, and nationalism, then at least *structural* racism, sexism, heterosexism, ableism, and nationalism.

But if the most prominent of these performances typically play to a narrow band of privileged audiences, what is their relation to the broader public sphere? Christopher Balme, in *The Theatrical Public Sphere*, offers a careful definition of Habermas's theory as it applies to the theater, worth quoting extensively:

> The defining feature of the bourgeois public sphere is reasoned discourse by private persons on questions of public interest with the aim of achieving rational consensus. It is characterized by almost universal access, autonomy (participants are free of coercion), equality of status (social rank is subordinated to quality of argument) and exchange of argument through rational-critical debate. Habermas's historical argument hinges on two transformations: from the feudal 'representative' public sphere to a bourgeois rational-critical one during the eighteenth century, and then to the degeneration of the latter in the late nineteenth and twentieth centuries under the influence of mass media, the commodification of culture, and the political manipulation of public opinion: 'a public sphere manufactured for show'.[15]

If access, autonomy, equality, and argument are the key features of the Habermasian public sphere, then we can easily see how idealized forms of democracy and democratic deliberation cohere around this construction of an idealized public sphere. To a certain degree, this is a utopian spatial construct (which we'll discuss below); but these outlines not only inform ideals, they inform political arguments about how both theater and politics should work, arguments that take place across the actual public sphere, which is messier and less just than Habermas's model typically acknowledges. Other models theorized by Arendt and Rawls also emerge as interlocutors in discussions of the public sphere, though neither is as direct about the role of theatrical storytelling in their conceptions.

In fact, Habermas's work in *The Structural Transformation of the Public Sphere* has been clear about the role that the theaters played in the cultivation of public spaces—literal and conceptual—for debating ideas, though Habermas focuses largely on the Enlightenment 18th century for these origins. The work of Paul Yachnin and others has focused specifically on the role of theater in making the private public in the early modern period, a key element of the construction of the public.[16] Balme locates those origins more distinctly in the anti-theatrical debates surrounding the English Commonwealth period, noting the "arena of debate conducted in countless pamphlets and tracts, on the stage and off, in courthouses and churches."[17] While Balme is clear about the historical role of the theater in Habermas's narrative of "structural transformation," he is also clear that we cannot be facile about theater's thoroughgoing participation in the public sphere, locating a retreat from real participation in public debate in the rise of the black box and the abolition of censorship, noting that in this context, "it is seldom the performance that contributes to the public sphere, but more often the theatre in its institutional function."[18]

Balme, therefore, is careful to define where the public sphere and theatrical performance diverge, and how, despite that divergence, convergences appear to place them back into conversation. He notes, for example, the legacy of agit-prop and Living Newspapers in participating in public debate, while comparatively disregarding aesthetic idealism, and adds that in our current moment, "genres such as verbatim theater follow similar strategies of using documents, real-life testimony, court cases, and parliamentary debates to draw attention to questions circulating in the public sphere."[19] But drawing attention to those questions is not the same as actually nurturing public debate. Balme maintains that "for all its modernist and postmodernist reclusivity, theatre remains a public space, albeit a highly modulated, even compromised one."[20] Is it possible, then, that in the hypermediatized neoliberal period, the thorough degradation of the rational-critical public sphere (already a century on, in Habermas's narrative), a "public sphere manufactured for show" in the form of a staged dialogue on matters of public interest, is the closest we could get in the last 40 years to an actual public dialogue of the sort Habermas valorizes?

• • •

Insofar as theater scholarship has taken up discussions of the public sphere to a certain degree, significant work on this concept has occupied the fields of political philosophy and political communication over the last 25 years. For example, Seyla Benhabib's work from 1996's *Democracy and Difference* onward has worked to theorize a pluralist public sphere in the context of an increasingly cosmopolitian society.[21] In a remarkable 1997 article, Benhabib identifies a central tension in conceptions of the public sphere (particularly Arendt, Habermas, and Rawls) around the sense of unity and unanimity assumed by the legitimation processes of public discourses (i.e., agreement to the terms of public reason and deliberation as a decision-making mechanism) and the boisterously multivocal and multicultural realities that drive much of the debate within today's public sphere. She argues for retaining a conception of the public sphere in face of "global capitalism [that appears] to generate communication without deliberation," but one that simultaneously opens up its conception of public deliberation to include the porous relationship between culture and politics, and a necessary though dangerous imperative to democratize participants in that public sphere while increasing the public capacity to engage public deliberation with sophistication and nuance.[22] "To recognize and come to grips with the implications of its own diversity," Benhabib insists, "a democratic people needs to reenact its identity in the public sphere," almost as if she was calling for more verbatim theater just as the form was approaching its fullest expression.[23]

Central to this critical conversation, then, is an understanding of what constitutes democratic public deliberation. Amy Gutmann and Dennis Thompson define deliberative democracy "as a form of government in which free and equal citizens (and their representatives) justify decisions in a process in which they give one another reasons that are mutually acceptable and generally accessible, with the aim of reaching conclusions that are binding in the present on all citizens but open to challenge in the future."[24] Gutmann and Thompson's definition succumbs to some of Benhabib's critiques, focusing primarily on institutional forms of government and the binding kinds of decision-making that happens there; but their focus on the *processes* of "giv[ing] one another reasons" links our understanding of the public sphere to democracy and its decision-making processes. Simone Chambers, however, makes the useful (and critical) distinction between deliberative democracy and democratic deliberation, noting that deliberation focuses in particular on "discrete deliberative initiatives *within* democracies," rather than the relationship of these deliberations to the state or actual decision-making.[25] What emerges in Chambers's critical reading of democratic deliberation is that because the public sphere is itself too complex and cacophonous to sustain mass-public dialogue, deliberation is reduced to micro-publics where the kinds of reenactments of public democracy of the sort Benhabib wishes for may appear, but which seem disconnected from actual decision-making, especially beyond the local level. I would historicize this gap from Benhabib's article in 1997 to Chambers's critique in 2009 by noting that in that time, documentary theater emerged from its most popular expressions into the boom of these forms in the middle of the Bush-Blair years, only to discover that these performances—successful theatrically—had little effect on policy or even public opinion.

In the meantime, the fields of political theory and communication have still taken up many of the key topics germane to a discussion of an idealized public sphere through staged democratic deliberation. Following Benhabib's *Democracy and Difference*, Iris Marion Young's *Inclusion and Democracy* lays out ways that deliberative democracy might be more inclusive: an implicit goal of many of the democratic dramaturgies of verbatim theater projects, and a hallmark in the field.[26] Further, several articles look at the roles of narrative in public deliberation in ways cognate with the story-telling approach of the oral history methodologies that populate these performances.[27] More recently, these discussions (particularly in political communications and rhetoric) have come to examine the roles of emotions and empathy in political debate, a subject I'll take up more directly in chapter 3.

What these conversations all share, however, is a commitment to democracy itself, along the lines of what Young identifies as "the operating conviction of this book [*Inclusion and Democracy*], that democratic practice is a means of promoting justice" and which underscores most of these scholars' commitment to deepening that democratic practice. And while I share that commitment generally, I also note the correspondence of the vociferousness of this commitment in both the theory and in the theater. At the same time, though, political theorist Jodi Dean notes that at least up through her retrospective reading of the Bush administration in 2009, *both* sides of our politically contested divide made persistent appeals to democracy, a symptom to her of a unified (and corrupt) political commitment to expanding neoliberal markets over "social justice and economic equality."[28] In Dean's reading, this frequent rhetorical appeal to democracy has slipped in to fill the void left by the collapse of Soviet socialism, supplementing an actually effective left politics with an infinitely deferred conception of democratic deliberation that stands in for actual political action. "Real existing constitutional democracies," she notes, "privilege the wealthy," as the right engages in market-centric political maneuvering underneath a middle-left posturing around democratic values.[29] Noting the same "gap between deliberation and decision" that Chambers notes, Dean asks pointedly, "if democracy is conceptualized in terms of deliberative procedures and practices of justification, in what way are the acts and decisions that evade and supplement these practices, democratic?"[30] This appeal, she concludes, "is a dead end for left politics."[31]

Dean is not eschewing democracy per se, but rather the political efficacy of the persistent *appeal* to democracy as a remedy for the economic and social inequalities maintained under neoliberalism. Instead, she points to a "reliance on democracy" as getting in the way of "envisioning another politics in the future."[32] Meanwhile, if the left has failed to envision another politics (which, given the more recent rise of a progressive left in the form of Bernie Sanders and Alexandria Ocasio-Cortez, is debatable), the right has been busy re-envisioning its own. Indeed, in the era of Trump, right-wing appeals to democracy have dried up, as undisguised voter suppression, gerrymandering, and persistent and unfounded invocations of what Atiba Ellis calls "the meme of voter fraud" has led vociferous Trump supporters on social media to return to the old chestnut that "we're not a democracy, we're a republic."[33] Republican (big-R and little-r) conceptions of governmental power have abandoned the goal of democracy as a radical socialist plot, even as radical socialists like Dean are questioning the appeal to democracy itself.

• • •

I was more sanguine when I first started writing about documentary and verbatim theater right at the millennium's break. Just finishing up a dissertation on life writing and feminist theater, I saw verbatim theater as a vehicle for both progressive feminist politics and form, even when the play's subject matter wasn't explicitly feminist.

I wrote that these performances encourage "the integration of the audience into the tenuous sense of community created by the theatrical event itself."[34] I suggested that the form shifted "focus from a linear subject-oriented trajectory to a multi-voiced community-oriented one."[35] I suggested that they "often seek to reveal a hidden truth to give voice to silenced voices or to expose what has been kept hidden."[36] I spent a good bit of time thinking through the construction of community, using the sociological concept of the *gemeinschaft*—a community built on actual interpersonal ties, rather than just market-based ones. Here, I also began to think through the way that dialogue and community functioned in ways that worked much like Balme imagines that the Habermasian public sphere might function in the theater. Onstage, this might be how "these plays often try to represent dialogue between . . . different communities, if not by representing actual dialogue, then by placing their monologues in close proximity to one another."[37] The representational result, I argued, was that the plays modeled the replacement of "singular, hegemonic voice with a dialogue of voices that presupposes a more democratic conception of power."[38]

This argument posits, as I do in this project, that these performances *represent* an idealized public sphere—participants given equal standing to air their positions in a form that looks like dialogue and rational exchange. I took an additional step, following Smith's own descriptions of post-play discussions, to suggest that this model public sphere initiated a real, functioning public sphere. Smith argued in the introduction to *Twilight*, "*I believe that solutions to these problems will call for large and eclectic groups of people.*"[39] This claim is precisely the appeal to deliberative democracy that Dean critiques, here inherent in the democratic dramaturgies of verbatim theater. And exactly from Smith's point, I argued that the goal of these performances was "to create in the audience a sense of community that encourages dialogue, that allows for the peaceful confrontation of individual identities and incorporates them all."[40] And the result? "A narrative theatrical experience that lays the groundwork for progressive political action through acknowledgement and consideration of the other through dialogue"[41] and that is "depatriarchalized and anti-hegemonic in comparison to the often-violent discourse" that these plays seek to remedy.[42]

It is difficult, perhaps impossible, to know how to gauge what I am experiencing in this critical, even suspicious reassessment of my own earlier thinking. While trying not to dismiss these arguments as naïve, I wonder: has the veil of optimism been lifted from my privileged eyes in these angrier times (am I just now coming to understand things that people of color, disenfranchised workers, LGBTQ+ people, or people with disabilities have understood for years?) or has another veil of cynical disillusionment been lowered? Either way, I understand performances like *Twilight: Los Angeles*,

1992 much differently than I did when I first saw Smith in 1997 or wrote about her in the years following. I still believe that these plays *sought* to stage an idealized public sphere onstage in order to enact one in the audience. I have doubts, though, that verbatim theater can do any such thing today.[43]

• • •

There is perhaps less to be said about plays like Smith's *Fires in the Mirror, Twilight: Los Angeles, 1992*, or Mann's *Greensboro: A Requiem* than the occasion to reassess might suggest. Each of these plays, as I argued in 2003, seeks to function just as I described. (Indeed, their connections are more than just incidental, since Mann directed *Twilight* at the Mark Taper Forum in LA, where it premiered.) Let me note, though, a few trends that show up in the text of the plays themselves, trends that largely underscore the particular fantasy of democratic deliberation engendered by this staged public sphere.

REPRESENTATIVE VOICES

Central to an imagined public sphere is the appearance of access to the space of debate and equalized status among those who are there. If anything, this quality is the hallmark of this style. In Mann's *Greensboro*, for example, about a massacre perpetrated by KKK members at a Marxist worker's rights event, Mann is careful to ensure that voices appear from both those who survived the event and those who perpetrated it. We hear from prominent KKK members such as David Duke as well as "local boys" who actually participated in the violent event. Smith's work is even more dedicated to this tactic: *Fires in the Mirror* and *Twilight: Los Angeles, 1992* are both populated by voices that represent communities in conflict, as well as those in various positions of power to mediate those conflicts. *Fires in the Mirror*, for example, develops its narrative with a fairly consistent back-and-forth of Lubavitcher and African American speakers, punctuated with appearances by more public figures like Reverend Al Sharpton or Angela Davis. But *Twilight* really sees this method develop. Robin Bernstein's reading of *Twilight* notes how centrally Smith situates this tactic within her approach: "In order to have real unity, all voices would have to first be heard or at least represented."[44] Not only do audiences hear from African American protestors and white police officials, we hear from Korean shop owners, Latinx artists, journalists, jurors, and cultural commentators—from academics like Homi Bhabha, Mike Davis, and Cornel West to outspoken celebrities like Jessye Norman and Charlton Heston (already then spokesperson for the NRA).[45] Indeed, so committed are many critics to the idea of equitable representation that Smith's penchant for staging celebrities has sometimes drawn criticism from those interested in ensuring that a pre-existing public persona doesn't grant unseemly access to her stage.[46]

PUBLIC OPINION VOICES

One upshot of this sense of access to the stage space of public deliberation is that "the public" is often represented on stage not just by less empowered voices, but also by voices who don't have a direct stake in the debate but who nonetheless represent public sentiment. Like the "little man" figure in Living Newspaper performances, these voices frame stances that might be widely held, particularly by audience members. These figures are not always present, and in the tribunal context of Greensboro, may be absent, except for in the figure of the interviewer who is staged gathering information and asking questions. In *Fires in the Mirror*, for example, Smith offers up two different "Anonymous Young Man" characters, whose opinions on the violent events of that play—the Crown heights riots of 1991—do not include direct testimony as to what happened, but express popular opinion about the landscape of the neighborhood and provide important insight into the tensions of that community. And consider Katie Miller, from *Twilight*. We learn little about Miller except that she is a bookkeeper from South Central and wears a baseball hat. We hear her reporting about the lootings happening in South Central and Koreatown, telling listeners about the way these lootings were covered on TV and in the newspapers, and what she found offensive about that reporting. Here, Miller stands in for residents of South Central, but also for media consumers who might have accessed these events only through these same media.[47] A public opinion figure may introduce red herrings into the discourse ("I didn't like the idea of them hittin' Pep Boys"), but very rarely are they represented as introducing falsehoods. And in the case of Miller, her "little man" persona serves to bracket and dilute the emphasis of more powerful voices, like Sharpton's.

These figures pop up across the genre, though, and hardly uniformly. When they do, they are often relegated to one-off appearances, sometimes at the beginning or end of an act; they show up, for example, in Soans's *Talking to Terrorists* and Brittain and Slovo's *Guantanamo*. But given the outsized role that the media plays in shaping public opinion—and more recently, the tyranny of public opinion as it develops and shapes the experience of social media—I wonder how much we should idealize these figures. In Living Newspaper performances of the 1930s, the "little man's" representation of public opinion stood as a counterbalance to power. And now we must begin to wonder if that figure in today's moment is subject to misinformation campaigns, or worse, is a troll or a bot. Today, we may be right to be suspicious, but these plays, we must remember, are *idealizations* of the public sphere, and as such, they idealize the intentions of its participants.

EVEN-HANDEDNESS AND NEUTRALITY

Even when a specific stance is comparatively evident, verbatim performances from this period often take on an air of objective neutrality. Smith's performances provide no framing for her monologues, so any editorializing is embedded in the selection and arrangement of the monologues themselves. Smith's cultivation of her ethos of neutrality is well-documented;[48] Bernstein in particular reads this warily, noting her "*supposed* neutrality," that "Smith has *encouraged* people to read her as unbiased," and that she "has *constructed* herself . . . a neutral ear or an empathic mirror."[49] Similarly, even when political sympathies are not particularly hidden, as in *Greensboro*, this representation of an even-handed approach to conflict was, in 1996, understood largely as a virtue, a method of locating larger structures of feeling rather than making tribunal style accusations. Vincent Canby's *New York Times* review of *Greensboro* notes, for example, that the play's "heart is with the victims, but the play is postmodern in its politics. It's less concerned with any 'isms' or parties than with the climate of ignorance and duplicity that made the confrontation inevitable."[50]

It is a particular pleasure to read here Canby's framing of these as postmodern politics, and also to re-encounter Robin Bernstein's work on Smith, especially since Bernstein is a scholarly contemporary who both locates great optimism in her reading of Smith's work, but does so with a subtle skepticism about Smith's claims to neutrality. Certainly, these plays were understood to live in the milieu of postmodernism, a milieu that may still linger, but which seems to have reached a punctuation mark on 9/11, the same mark Raymond Geuss identifies for the beginning of the end of the Habermasian public sphere. What is crucial for me to understand and to point out here, is that 25 years ago we all knew that neutrality was impossible, and we all (in different ways) rolled our eyes at these declarations of objective even-handedness. But I also understood (at least implicitly) that *the appearance* of neutrality was the thing, that this appearance was a precondition to the invitation into the room to deliberate meaningfully.

OPEN-ENDEDNESS

If an upshot of the performance of equal access to the deliberative space to the documentary stage is a purported even-handed neutrality, a further extension is a refusal to draw conclusions—a theatrical process designed to look more like discussion than like prosecution. Open-endedness connects to the imagined efficacy of these performances: that deliberation is not simply modeled on stage but is catalyzed by that model. If the theater is to perform a public sphere into existence, then it must leave open the space for conversations to continue, and so formal closure becomes an obstacle to that goal. The tribunal play, by contrast, often must end on a clear note, in which juridical deliberation has been completed and a verdict is clear—whether the "correct" verdict occurred historically or not. Feminist critics have long theorized narrative closure as a feature of hegemonic storytelling; the logic is that patriarchy forecloses options for women by foreclosing the possibilities of their stories. I maintain that this critique extends to the anti-authoritarian work of public-sphere documentary theater too: that "writing beyond the ending," to borrow Rachel Blau DuPlessis's term, keeps deliberation open, creating new possibilities for something like liberatory discourse. DuPlessis, too, notes the communal as a key strategy, and the community-focused elements of these performances underscore a sense that democratic deliberation can be a remedy to hierarchical power.[51]

This transition from the case-closed format of the tribunal to the opening-out of ongoing community cultural work emerges in *Greensboro*. The play ends with African American minister and massacre-survivor Nelson Johnson, speaking to white ministers in his community: "I told them: I made the first step. Now it's up to you—up to all of us—we got to turn these people, your people, *around*."[52] The projection screen reads, "First step" and then fades and tells the audience of the outcome of the verdict, that

"In 1985, for the first time in American legal history, local police and the Ku Klux Klan were found jointly liable in a wrongful death. The city of Greensboro paid the judgment for the police. No Klan or Nazi member has paid the judgment."[53] While audiences learn the final outcome, they are simultaneously charged by the character of Nelson with doing further cultural work, a move clearly called a *first*, and not *last* step. By keeping a sense of closure at bay, Mann seems to be trying to keep open the space for deliberation, and—despite the fact that the events it narrated were already 17 years old when the play premiered—a sense that their consequences still warrant deliberation and further action.

Similarly, Smith often disrupted linear sequence merely by juggling the "set list" of monologues in *Twilight*, substituting in and out different monologues, changing their order, etc. But she frequently ended with gang truce organizer Twilight Bey's monologue, a monologue that associates the character's name with an in-between-ness, a state where light and darkness coexist. The monologue is hardly explicit on the events of the play at all, even as the character advocates for the end of gang violence and expresses worry about the way that drugs turn the lives of individuals upside down. But in ruminating on the notion of "twilight" itself, the monologue advances the idea that in-between and grey areas are places where people from different identities can meet and begin to understand one another. There's no narrative closure in this moment; in fact, barely any narrative at all. By ending on an ambiguous note, the performance presses toward an ongoing dialogue.

AFFECTIVE INFORMATION

While Habermas's public sphere is a space for rational deliberation, we must recognize that in this iteration, affective information is crucial to the performance. How these crises *feel* to individuals is as important as—and sometimes more important than—the ways that rational frameworks of state apparatuses might determine outcomes. Or, as Lauren Berlant puts it, "Public spheres are always affect worlds, worlds to which people are bound, when they are, by affective projections of a constantly negotiated common interestedness."[54] While I will discuss the role of empathy in this construction in chapter 3, it is worth noting here that the idealized public sphere is not populated simply by reasoned arguments, but also by felt emotional appeals. Empathetic listening is connected to impartial and fair listening in the ideal communicative situation of the public sphere, but empathy itself is not typically posed as crucial to democratic deliberation. In these plays, though, and perhaps as importantly in the *criticism* of these performances, it is the key, as Della Pollock notes, to enacting change. This ethic of empathetic listening comes into view when interviewers, and sometimes the playwrights themselves, become listening interlocutors. The trope of the site of the interview, and often even the interviewer-as-character, is a common occurrence in these performances. In Smith's work, which only ever stages the performer embodying the interviewee, audiences still hear references to the context of the interview itself, the site for listening. Mann's *Greensboro* stages the interviewer as a regular character who stands in, at least in part, for public opinion. And we can see the phenomenon appearing across the genre—taken to almost neurotic extremes, for example, when Doug Wright in *I Am My Own Wife* stages himself as a character whose deliberation over the ethics of the interview is almost as much a part of the plot as the life of the play's interview subject.

But the importance of affective information is not just that there is an empathetic listener, but that the emotional content is submitted—endorsed by the very editing and selection processes that create these performances—as a crucial component of the arguments that characters are making. That is to say, when we come across monologues or dialogue that are "moving," as many reviewers are quick to note, this content seems to be the ideally productive nexus of the theatrical public sphere. Perhaps because these plays are not simply about issues worthy of deliberation, but often implicitly about the legitimacy of the deliberators themselves, what they frame as at stake is not just access to the sphere of debate, but more to the point, access to *understanding*. This is the theatrical answer to a persistent critique of the Habermasian public sphere: that it does not theorize listening across difference. Social theorist Lincoln Dahlberg notes this critique, but also argues that *as an idealization* of political discourse, the public sphere is a perfect construct to theorize argumentation across difference, even as in practice the power dynamics in play may limit that idealization.[55] Similarly, in *Inclusion and Democracy*, Iris Marion Young writes:

> "Public Communication covers not only making claims and giving reasons, though this is and ought to be a significant aspect. It also includes politicized art and culture—film, theatre, song, and story—intended to influence a wider public to understand the society or some of its members in particular

> and often different ways. If public communication aims at inclusion, debate, and promoting justice, furthermore, it must include multiple forms of protest action."[56]

Even as these social theorists articulate a broader shape for the public sphere to include other voices, they also acknowledge that "making claims and giving reasons" does not encompass the entirety of the public sphere's deliberative mechanisms. As I will explore later, emotion, and in particular empathy, has more recently emerged as a way to communicate, listen, and understand across difference.[57] In this way, as idealizations of the public sphere, particularly when identity-based difference is at stake, affective arguments take their place alongside rational ones. The spectacle presented here of idealized public deliberation, of empathetic listening across difference, becomes the particular domain of the theatricalized public sphere.

In these performances from the 1990s, especially, the introduction of affective information connects specifically to the ways in which participants in this public deliberation are accepted as speaking subjects in the deliberative field. In *Greensboro*, not surprisingly, we hear a fair amount of discourse about anger. Survivor Floris Weston, for example, delivers a monologue just before the reenactment of a scene from the civil trial after the massacre, noting "I guess I haven't dealt with a lot of the anger;" "I didn't know where to place my anger;" and "I suppose I'm most angry at the police."[58] This affective response becomes evidence for the audience to consider as they witness the civil trial. Even later on, Klansman Edward Dawson, largely framed as something of an ignorant dupe in the play, responds to the (unstaged) question about his *feelings* about the events: "How do I feel about that now? I feel like I was some kinda jerk." Dawson's understatement in the moment, his failed empathy for the lives lost, is similarly important information for the audience to consider as they make judgements over the legacy of this racist political violence.

Anger functions similarly in Smith's work, as she selects monologues that ask audiences to understand the anger that communities felt in the events that she re-performs. In a monologue that opens the published version of *Twlight*, for example, artist Rudy Salas Sr. tells a story of his son having a cop pull a gun on him, an echo of experiences Salas himself had: "How you think / a / father feels, / stuff that happened to me / fifty years / ago / happened to my son? / Man!"[59] And fatherhood makes a different kind of appearance in *Fires in the Mirror*, when Carmel Cato, father of the boy whose death sparked the Crown Heights Riots, tells the audience, "That's what's devastating me right now. / Sometime it make me feel like it's no justice."[60] Justice, here and in each of these other plays considered here, is connected to *feeling*, not just to argumentation. And as chapter 4 will explore, the feelings of democratic deliberation—that anger has been heard, that justice might be acted upon, that hope might be redeemed in change—were crucial to the construction of these plays in a moment in our recent history when we (or maybe just I?) believed that belief in one's common humanity might be the missing ingredient to reaching consensus on positive change.

• • •

When I say that this belief feels utopian now, I recognize that it has always been utopian, and in the next chapter, I will consider the space of utopian thinking and performing glimpsed by these plays. But imagining that space as an idealized public sphere—that the shape of utopia for a time took the form of space for democratic deliberation—is itself an historical construction, one particular to a neoliberal period in which the tenets of democratic deliberation required the affirmative assertion of artistic representation against—what?—the racist, sexist, and homophobic legacies of a time before the Civil Rights movement or second-wave feminism or Queer Nation? the encroachment of late capitalist logic into every criterion of human valuation? the emerging rationale of global empire under the guise of "freedom"? Yes, of course, all of these. And now that they have coalesced into a series of regimes worldwide that embrace domination and exclusion as necessary and even valuable expressions of an apparently laudable will to power, I wonder whether a public sphere is even imaginable. Yet as these plays suggest, until fairly recently the *forms* of democratic deliberation made for important theater, which asserted that beyond simply prosecuting plain injustice, the theater made space to consider what constitutes justice, and justice for whom.

2

Debating in Utopia

Sometime near the end of the last Bush administration, I delivered a talk at a regional conference of oral historians on the theme of oral history in performance. Although my talk was already on the subject of space and place, I was surprised to see how many of the conference participants had centered place in their own work—projects conceived not just around communities or groups of people, but specifically rooted in place—collectively performing or presenting on stories from Montreal; New Orleans; Blacksburg, Virginia; a whole borough's worth of stories from New York City. Central to many of those oral history projects were the acts of violence that engendered them: violently suppressed civil rights protests, hate crimes, terrorist acts and anti-terrorist responses, school massacres. And even when a single act of violence was not the impetus of the project, whole systems of micro-acts of violence—racism, xenophobia, sexism, homophobia—served as both catalysts and targets of what were the necessarily political inflections of these oral history performances. Of course, a quick skim over the then-developing canon of such performances would have revealed a similarly high rate of place names right in the titles: Crown Heights, Los Angeles, Greensboro, Laramie, Guantánamo.

These last two, I'll mention most often in this chapter—Moisés Kaufman and Tectonic Theater Projects' *The Laramie Project* (1999) and Victoria Brittain and Gillian Slovo's Tricycle Theatre-produced *Guantanamo: 'Honor Bound to Defend Freedom'* (2004)—because they highlight specific effects from two particular moments in the history of verbatim theater. But as particularly prominent entries in this form, they both stage place in the ways that have become familiar to audiences who follow documentary theater and its frequent tendencies toward minimal staging and "talking head" performance tactics. I see these tendencies as not just idiosyncrasies of the form, but as inextricably tied to the affective experience of a utopian public sphere that these plays seem inevitably trying to conjure.

In particular, three things strike me about the way that these pieces often imagine themselves as reparative events to create dialogue in response to violence. First is that they imagine themselves as public spheres in a particularly *spatial* sense. The second is that a functioning public sphere was itself seen as a reparative conceptual space, as much the ends themselves as the means to the ends. The third, the logical extension, is that in modeling public deliberation, these performed public spheres take the shape of deliberative utopias set in the same place as dystopian violence. That is to say, the violence endemic to a specific place is a frequent if not constant feature of such performances, which then must juxtapose the dystopian logic of much social critique with what Jill Dolan has called "utopian performatives," which, in her words, "allow fleeting contact with . . . a utopia always in process, always only partially grasped, as it disappears before us around the corners of narrative and social experience."[1]

It is worth considering how the sum of these premises—that a performance of a deliberative public sphere can enact utopian performatives—imagines all three concepts in spatial terms: occupying a performance space, representing a public sphere, inhabiting utopia. Habermasian theories of the public sphere are, of course, already spatial in the very term. Yet even though we know we are not talking about a literal sphere, it is difficult not to imagine participants stepping into a single space to participate in the lively exchange of ideas. And this public sphere is a space in the sense that it is not a place, exactly—the public sphere may be rooted to place, but its public deliberations might themselves seem to occur in a vacuum. In this way, the *emptiness* of the performance space becomes germane—the theater stage is already imagined as a conceptually empty space in which another place might be represented. How apt, then, that at their most optimistic about the power of political theater, theaters might have wanted to pull the conceptual framework of a public sphere onto the empty stage. Dolan, for example, uses the term "public sphere" twice in her chapter on *The Laramie Project*: first that the play "creat[es] a new public sphere in which to scrutinize the events leading up to and following [Matthew] Shepard's death," suggesting the way in which the play must imagine *its own self-contained space* for public deliberation. Later, that "I fervently wish for the theater to claim its place as a vital part of the public sphere," a notation that the public sphere created by the play does not necessarily connect directly to the "real public sphere of contemporary politics."[2] How much more apt, then, that theaters use the empty space of the stage to enact the most idealized version of deliberation we can imagine, even as we wish theater's utopian performative version were closer to the center of an actual public sphere that drives public discourse. I would argue, though, that the very utopian impulse of this idealized space—utopian and therefore etymologically *no-place*—helps us to understand the kind of spatial clearing-the-decks involved in envisioning this sort of deliberation.

I have never been entirely interested in what glimpses of future utopia these performances offered us, although I often believed in them, in very much the way that Dolan articulates. But I also realize a central tension existing along all of these layers, in that each utopian layer is repairing a dystopia by staging heterotopia.[3] That is, in order for us to imagine the public sphere functioning in an ideal way, we must begin with a problem situated in place, and invite dissenting speakers to share the common stage—deliberative utopia depends on real problems in real places that are undergirded by real disagreements. Place, in the case of these performances, appears in the form of the subject matter: the Laramies and Guantánamos of verbatim performance. In contrast, space is not the setting signified through theatrical representation, but rather the spaces of representation and of reception found in the theater itself. In fact, while the impulse of verbatim performance toward speech claims a particular representational purchase on the real, the form's conception of space is almost purely imaginative. It is a thinly representational abstraction, that, in its utopian leanings, is in fact vaguely fantastical. In order to reconcile the particular cities, towns, neighborhoods, and communities that give rise to verbatim performances, we must contend with the once-empty but now-bodied spaces of the stage and the theater and determine precisely how the theater seeks to serve as a mechanism for repairing the monologic violence of the dystopia into a glimpse of the political utopia by hosting a deliberative heterotopia. In doing so, we will see some of the ambivalences of invoking theatrical utopias in troubled political times.

Della Pollock suggests the particular promise of oral history in performance: that it "will be redeemed in some kind of change" and that "it catches its participants—often by surprise—in a contract with possibility: with imagining what might be, could be, should be."[4] These are precisely the terms with which Dolan talks about theatrical utopias. Dolan writes, "Performance's simultaneity, its present-tenseness, uniquely suits it to probing the possibilities of utopia as a hopeful process that continually writes a different, better future."[5] She further notes, "The very present-tenseness of performance lets audiences imagine utopia not as some idea of future perfection that might never arrive, but as brief enactments of the possibilities of a process that starts now, in this moment in the theatre."[6] I am struck particularly by the degree to which both writers describe these potentials in "processual" terms—that is, they mark them in time far more than in space.[7] Dolan simply notes that "Performance's . . . spatiality often anchors it to *an imagined place*, a 'what if' of matter and expression, but performance always exceeds its space and its image, since it lives only in its doing, which is imagining, in *the good no-place* that is theatre."[8] We should note Dolan's struggle with the spatiality of the utopian performative, for as she displaces spatiality into that "good no-place," she cites both the place of theatrical setting and the space of the theater itself. Here I find the peculiarity of spatial imagination of oral history performances, often firmly anchored *not* to an imaginary place, but rather to a materially, historically, and geographically specific place—a dystopian place, a place rooted in violence. And while Dolan notes that "spectators might draw a utopian performative from even the most dystopian theatrical universe," I think we must ask about this mechanism in the experiential shift from the dystopian places of Guantánamo, Laramie, or Crown Heights to the utopian space of the theater, and what that mechanism can elide in the places of performance.[9]

I am thinking through space and place here with Michel de Certeau and Yi-Fu Tuan. De Certeau imagines place in terms of "the order . . . with which elements are distributed in relationships of coexistence," that by determining place as relative to other stable elements—both material and (as Tuan points out) historical—place "implies an indication of stability."[10] This indication of stability applies, too, to the places of oral history: take, for example, the site of Rodney King's beating in Los Angeles, where the historical and physical situation of video-camera, bodies and batons lock that moment into a specific site of memory. This appearance of stability is just as clear in our imagination of a fencepost outside Laramie, Wyoming, or in imagining Guantánamo, where prisoners are (still), in fact, incarcerated into stable places, defined in relation to the boundaries of their cells by physical force, in relation to one another by their separation, and in relation to state power by their subordination. "Space" on the other hand "is composed of intersections of mobile elements. . . . In contradistinction to the place," de Certeau asserts, "it has thus none of the univocity or stability of a 'proper.' In short, *space is a practiced place*."[11] The dystopian settings of these verbatim performances are stable, defined by the co-existence of objects, bodies, and history in some ordered relation of a representational elsewhere and elsewhen. The theatrical space of performance is, by contrast, marked by possibility, as the rehearsal of "place" for utopia, glimpsed in the here and now of the audience, and as an opening for an ideally functioning public sphere, a formally frictionless conversation in which (in concept) ideas and values might float to the surface.

This distinction between the place represented and the space in which representation occurs suggests a particular phenomenology of theatrical space, in which we become, momentarily at least, less interested in representations than in the experiences they engender. Bert O. States writes that the elsewhere of theater "is not a spatial elsewhere in the sense that the mind thinks of being elsewhere . . . but in a sense that what is before us . . . offers a different kind of here than we 'usually tend to be' in."[12] So, if the stage of the verbatim performance is a different kind of here, we might ask beyond the obvious fact that we are not in the city of our theater (experientially), we are in, say, Laramie. More than this, we are not in the Laramie in which homophobia produced the murder of a young man, but one in which the conditions of speech itself make for a different kind of here. Stanton B. Garner Jr. goes even further: "On one hand, the field of performance is scenic space, given as spectacle to be processed and consumed by the perceiving eye, objectified as field of vision for a spectator who aspires to the detachment inherent in the perceptual act."[13] The spectacle, then, is the field inhabited by characters, the representational elsewhere that invokes place. "On the other hand," he continues, "this field is environmental space, 'subjectified' (and intersubjectified) by the physical actors who body forth the space they inhabit." In this way, Garner argues, "theatrical space is phenomenal space."[14] As such, the environmental space of the theater doesn't exclude the audience from the representation, as the representational, scenic space does, but rather, "includes the audience, which is situated in the phenomenological continuum of space through physical proximity, linguistic inclusions, and the uniquely theatrical mirroring that links audience with performer in a kind of corporeal mimetic identification."[15] Phenomenal space ends up including both the different elsewhere of verbatim-Laramie (which is itself a Laramie with smoothed out and controlled conditions for speaking and listening), as well as the present, experiential world of the audience. Together these become a brief, tightly controlled, highly idealized public sphere, one that incorporates the audience into its deliberations, but only within the ordered world of the playwright's organization. Utopia indeed.

Yet against this no-place, verbatim performances are often *defined* by real geographical place, and often as well by real historical time.[16] The referents of Laramie or Guantánamo are both physically elsewhere, and temporally else*when*, yet somehow, these performances seek both to be physically *present* and temporally *present-oriented,* always working toward the phenomenal. This is the paradox of these performances: presenting a specific and violent past rooted in place, yet never entirely retreating into the scenic field of representation, still determinedly existing within the experiential space of the audience. We do not feel transported to Guantánamo in the Tricycle Theatre production of the same name, where wrongfully imprisoned write their letters home, but rather that they have come to our theater—the space of future possibility and present experience—to talk to us. Voices are uprooted from the dystopias of "then and there" and resituated in the potentially utopian "here and now," what Dolan calls that "good no-place that is theater," a space that we know is always on the verge of transformation, with every new set, every light cue, every new audience. The utopian space that is performed here, then, is not simply a glimpse of transformative change, but also (we must acknowledge) the virtually impossible utopian deliberative space that has been opened up in the experiential present—a set of discursive conditions for a public sphere that in reality rarely survive out in the wild of public discourse.

So, when these performances effect a shift toward phenomenal space while still staging representational place, they typically do so by performing the geographical and historical setting in a way that we might describe as "thin" or "vague." Understanding that "place" depends upon the coexistence of elements in fixity, then verbatim performances have typically avoided this fixity by refusing to populate the spatial field of the theater with other representational objects tied to place. And because representational objects are absent in the performance space, these performances can stay in the experiential space of the audience (and at the same time, invoke utopias of possibility). Markers of place populate the field of performance in specifically calibrated ways: in the scene and set, in staged bodies, in the documents that define documentary dramaturgies, and in configurations of language and voice specific to verbatim modes. Thus, *The Laramie Project* and *Guantanamo: 'Honor Bound to Defend Freedom'*—in their specific historical moments—were able to show audiences these configurations of place in ways that particularly enabled the *feeling* in the theater of participating *now* in a utopian public sphere, and not just glimpsing a distant future utopia.

We can begin looking at these productions by looking directly at the sets themselves. The commonplace to think of sets in documentary theater as minimal holds true here. When audiences do see place represented, we get the *suggestion* of place, more than specific mimetic design. In particular, two types of places are often invoked (or meaningfully elided): the site of the interview and the site of violence itself. We see the site of violence less often, for a number of reasons; the site of the interview ends up being a safer space to stage for all of the reasons that verbatim theater could be invested with the hope of political change in these years. As Pollock notes, "the oral history interview lifts what might otherwise dissolve into the ephemera of everyday life onto the plane of ongoing exchange and meaning-making, infusing it with the power of shifting relationships among tellers and listeners."[17] Precisely this perception of anti-hierarchical process has keyed a belief in the progressive and anti-hegemonic impulses of the form, impulses that are central to imagining a smoothly functioning staged public deliberation. And importantly, this investment in anti-hierarchical process has appeared to stand in direct contrast to the dysfunctional power relationships that engendered both these particular moments of extraordinary physical violence and systems of discursive violence that underpin them.

The *New York Times*'s Jesse McKinley calls this "you-are-there theater" but it might more reasonably be imagined as "together, we are nowhere," because place is invoked in such a minimal way, and a way that is obviously an index to place, rather than a particular representation.[18] The off-Broadway production of *The Laramie Project*'s set, designed by Robert Brill, consisted largely of a black brick wall, several straight-backed chairs, and a sliding wall used as a projection screen.[19] Brill, who also designed the Mark Taper Forum production of Smith's *Twilight: Los Angeles, 1992*, solidified a design aesthetic that has become something of the default starting point for these productions, and for several good reasons. The design framework (in Brill's design and in untold other verbatim productions since) is typically set in Garner's "phenomenal space;" when stagings have invoked place, they tend to invoke the scene of the interview or other communicative exchange:

chairs become incredibly important to the design. The background space is almost never particularly referential, and projection screens facilitate an indexical pointer to the changing of place rather than serving as backdrop per se. The blankness of set encourages a flexibility of the production of presentation space, keeping the action free to exist within the environmental space of the audience and the actors.[20]

Guantánamo, even more rooted in dystopian place, similarly uses a fairly bare stage for its set, but works in somewhat more complex fashion. In the 2005 production that I saw at Washington, DC's Studio Theatre (which basically followed the original Tricycle Theatre staging), the stage was divided into three sections: the apron, from which actors playing officials like Donald Rumsfeld would recreate public statements and press conferences; the mid-stage area, which contained most of the actual oral history material gathered from detainees' families, and which, like these other performances, only vaguely referenced a minimalist scene of the interview through tables and chairs; and finally, the upstage area, representing the detention facility itself. This last space was the most explicitly referential, with prison beds and caging to mark off the spaces of individual prisoners whose often-censored letters form the basis for their speech. In this representational section of the performance, dystopia was most explicitly invoked, largely through the specific references to place. Furthermore, the public spaces from which power spoke (Rumsfeld's press conferences being the most obvious example) invoked a similarly dystopian dynamic, where those in power refused to engage in dialogue. Importantly, then, the space in which the particulars of the oral history exchange (rather than public statements or censored letters) were re-played were bounded behind by the prison and in front by those in power. Accordingly, the audience's access to the phenomenal spaces of oral history at mid-stage were disrupted by incursions of power and framed by the specter of discipline. These persistent invocations of dystopia mitigated the utopian performatives that might have been in play, but also provided a conceptual critique of the limits of that utopian deliberative impulse, revealing in particularly spatial arrangements the way that deliberation can be both contained, censored, and pre-empted by the official workings of power.

Even so, the verbatim set has tended to allow place to recede to the background, functioning often at most as symbolic spectre of violence that replaces a representation of place. Into this thinly represented place, then, the co-existence of bodies on stage and in the theater, and the ways in which those bodies hail one another, create new spatial dynamics for the performance. There are multiple vectors to consider here: for example, Garner emphasizes bodies as particularly present in the phenomenological field, one that simultaneously includes spectators, actors and characters. When actors address the audience directly, they affirm their presence in the experiential space of the present, and in doing so, interpellate the audience into the dialogue presented onstage, engaging them as active listeners, and bodying forth the communicative sphere which defines the utopian dimension of oral history performance. That is, while Garner notes that the intersubjectivity of theater occurs in the phenomenal, experiential space of the theater, Dolan locates the creation of utopian performatives particularly in moments of intersubjectivity. I, too, in this period argued that the utopian *communitas* of oral history theater derived precisely from this mechanism by which the audience could imagine themselves in dialogue with the speakers onstage, an imaginative act facilitated by the sense of presence within the experiential field.[21] Here, performance behavior is linked with both experience and presence, and delivered to the audience in a way that is both directly *experiential* in the intersubjective moment of direct address, and firmly *present,* in that the performer's direct address comes alive in the phenomenal space of audience witnessing.[22]

Conversely, the degree to which characters interact with one another on stage calls into being "place" by using the representational space between them *as distance*, especially when they interact in character. In doing so, the actors' bodies re-instantiate themselves as symbolic materiality: the actorly body gives way to the character, and with that signification of multiple characters in space comes the relational stability that de Certeau associates with place. In instances like this, *The Laramie Project* strategically stages place by representing the interviewer/ performers interacting with the citizens of Laramie *in Laramie*. Much of the play is performed with characters in isolation; characters are introduced to the audience early on by a narrator who affirms the presence of these voices in the experiential space of the theater, and even when multiple voices are interspersed with one another, they seem not to be directly interacting, leaving the representational context of Laramie only very thinly visible. But when Stephen Belber the character interviews Zubaida Ula the character, we get a performance of the scene *in Laramie* in which Stephen Belber the person interviewed Zubaida Ula the person. Similarly, a phone call in historical time between cast member Amanda Gronich and the Baptist minister's wife invokes distance in terms of both those two characters' ideological positions, and also in terms of physical space, by the distance implied in a telephone conversation. But while these do represent some sense of Laramie in the aftermath of the killing of Matthew Shepard, this is a Laramie depicted as moving decidedly toward dialogue, a movement that we are led to believe is in part spurred on by the presence of the interviewers. In fact, many of the moments represented within scenic space are moments of the oral history interview itself, moments that have utopian overtones in their re-situation of memory into seemingly deliberative dialogue.[23]

Other moments in *The Laramie Project* that directly invoke both the past and place of dystopia involve the use of documentation other than oral history. Here, *Laramie* and plays like it show their affinity with other forms of documentary theater. Reproducing media reportage (often presented onstage with video monitors or TV cameras), police and medical documents (in the off-Broadway production, projected onto a sliding wall), and court transcripts (which play out in re-enactments of courtroom scenes), the play presents evidence documented through various technologies: camera, audio recording, court transcriptions. These technologies, while certainly part of the oral history exchange, diminish the presence of the oral historian as human witness while simultaneously invoking the "real," moving from subjective memory to objective accuracy. Carol Martin confirms this, noting that technology is "necessary for the verification of the factual accuracy of both text and performance," and that "adherence to an archive makes documentary theatre appear closer to actuality than fiction."[24] Setting aside the issues of fact and actuality that Martin and others incisively take up, I am more interested in the ways that these technologically-reproduced bits of evidence, through their appearance of reliability, more concretely seem to represent the "real," and through it, the fixed places from which they were gathered.

Similarly, in *Guantanamo*, while interviews with family members of detainees are gathered through oral history methodologies, and invite a sense of dialogue, both the press conference material and the censored words of the inmates come from specific documents, presented accordingly. Cameras and reporters are placed in the audience for the official speeches, which has the curious effect of distancing audience members conceptually, even from space in the theater that they inhabit. Meanwhile, actors playing prisoners read their own letters from the space of their cells upstage, while certain words are silenced by an amplified voice declaring "Censored" over specific language. In each of these cases, the self-conscious presentation of documentation calls attention to the representational world of violence and power and encourages a lingering sense of dystopia, reproducing the imprisonment of place more fully than it admits the potentialities of space.

Speech itself, then, emerges to exist specifically within the experiential space of the audience, particularly under specific linguistic conditions. Consider Garner's discussion of *deixis*, the linguistic and representational pointing in words like "here" and "now," and in the physical reference of present objects and bodies to symbolic objects and bodies in the world of the narrative. In particular, deictic language constructs the *mise-en-scène*: "Although person (and the other deictic elements) function referentially, inscribing situations and participants of actual utterance in discourse," he says, "they do so only to the extent to which those situations and participants are already staged in language. The act of utterance, in a sense, is always preceded by a field of relationship intrinsic to discourse itself."[25] So while verbatim performance does not often specifically refer, through pronouns and direct language, to the space of the theater, it does often refer to the site of violence, the place of the play, in deictically other terms: using the past tense, and relying on pronouns like "there" and "then." Consider the moment in *The Laramie Project* entitled "The Fence," referring to the specific place where Shepard was beaten and left to die. While other moments in *Laramie* reference place in specific ways as a site for potential transformation—the possibility of growing dialogue in the community—the fence itself is always Other. Each interview describes a moment in past tense—visits to the site, the discovery of Shepard's body by a cyclist, the removal of the body by the first police officer on the scene. One character refers to the fence as "that place." The fence is never shown as part of the representational space of the scene; while images may be projected, none of the action of the play takes place there. This place is irretrievably a site of violence, and the language used to describe it, therefore, distances it from the space of the theater. It is a "there," and a "then," and it is spoken about by the characters in precisely the same terms of distance as it would be spoken about by the audience in the here and now—the same here and now occupied by the audience.

What is here and now about these plays, what opens up the space of the theater to experience, is the speech act itself. The verbatim form revolves around the exchange of speech, and its emphasis on voice reorients us to the space of the theater *as a public sphere*. As Garner says, "Dramatic language is infused with the speaking present."[26] Speech becomes the theatrical focus;

utterance, in the time and space of the present and of presence, invokes the theater itself—a world brought forth by language and bodies in space. Under these conditions, utopia is most persistently glimpsed, in the possibility for communication, for transformation. When the father of detainee Moazzam Begg expresses puzzlement about his son's detention, he speaks to us as stand-ins for the interviewer, but also as ourselves; he seems to be coming to us to question modes of power. And when Moisés Kaufman recounts his experiences interviewing the residents of Laramie, he is recounting them, his own and his interviewees' memories of a trauma revisited, to his audiences.

• • •

If these performances are able to create a spatialized utopia by *thinning out* the places of violence they are representing, and doing so in order to draw the bodies of actors and audience together in the "here and now" of the phenomenal space of the theater, I note that this maneuver depends to a certain degree on clearing out the place-based histories of the performance space itself as well. What does it mean, then, to create a utopian public sphere, if it depends upon erasing the histories not just of the place represented, but also the place in which representation occurs? If staging discussion depends on the no-place of the stage, what tools do we have to engage the messier realities of the histories of places staged, and places where stages are?

• • •

HISTORY, PLACE, AND VERBATIM PERFORMANCE: TWO ANECDOTES

Although I had just moved away from the Washington, DC, area when *Guantanamo* came to the Studio Theatre in fall 2005, I returned there to see the play and review the performance for *Theatre Journal.* Though the play is in many ways a British play—it focuses on a group of detainees who were British citizens, specifically, but it's also quite British in the way that most of Tricycle's tribunal productions held on to a bit of the agit-prop tradition—seeing the play *in place* in Washington, DC, was meaningful, particularly because the policies that governed that play's action were authored just down the street. We were still living under the Bush administration; Rumsfeld, portrayed on the stage that night, still ran the Pentagon, less than five miles to the south; we were still more than three years away from Obama's executive order to shutter the camp, when nearly 200 men still were detained there—though crucially, not the Tipton Three who were the subject of the play.[27] Those men, for whom *Guantanamo* was advocating, had been released, and because the play hinged largely (though not exclusively) on the injustices heaped upon those particular men, the play felt defused in general, but particularly so in Washington, DC, where not all of the audience (indeed, likely not many of them) favored the Bush policy around "enemy combatants." As I wrote then: "The Studio Theatre audience was as likely to be actively combating abuses of international law and human rights as they were to be complicit in those abuses. Yet with neither a conversation to enter nor an action to take, I left the theatre feeling accused rather than engaged."[28]

For all of its dematerializing of the dystopian space of the camp itself, the play couldn't bring us in together into space in a way that did not also elide the fact that this audience and this theater existed in a particular place, and in a particular moment. Its narrow utopia for theatrical deliberation seemed to collapse under the weight of the place it invoked, the place in which it was performed, and the history it staged. Even if it helps us glimpse a dialogue about detainment, it certainly didn't help us envision a grander view of how these stories might be redeemed in change. But then again, even after Obama's order in 2009, the complete emptying of Camp X-Ray at Guantánamo Bay Naval Base never occurred. Eight years later, as Obama prepared to leave the Oval office, forty detainees remained incarcerated there, even as the president-elect promised that "we're gonna load it up with some bad dudes, believe me."[29]

● ● ●

My new home is just an hour southeast of Laramie, Wyoming. Not surprisingly, that town is still no queer utopia, though what it is seems to be complicated. By accounts from within Laramie, it is a place changed, to be sure, but it is difficult to know what public deliberation has accomplished. Nationally, the Matthew Shepard Act was signed into law 11 years after Shepard's death (coincidentally, Obama signed it into law in the same year that he signed his initial executive order about Guantánamo). Locally, it's harder to know what has changed, a question taken up by *The Laramie Project: Ten Years Later*, which I will discuss some in the coda to this book. On the one hand, many acknowledge that the town is an important, if grudging, spot in the history of LGBTQ+ rights—young LGBTQ+ people growing up there are aware that it has shaped their own sense of their identities.[30] And yet some reports suggest that outward awareness has changed little about local attitudes:

> "How did the people of Laramie respond to the most significant event in the town's history? Many local officials and community leaders expressed outrage at the time of the tragedy but have stubbornly resisted efforts to erect a suitable memorial there. Residents of this neighborhood have been especially anxious to bury the past and even petitioned local government to change the street names in order to confuse pilgrims to the murder site."[31]

This current state of affairs in Laramie prompts me to ask whether this performance was (as Dolan suggests) a utopian rehearsal for the future, or a wishfully performed memorial in a place where little physical memorial can be found.

I took my first drive to Laramie in the late spring. A single highway connects my home in Fort Collins, Colorado to Laramie, and the 65 miles between might largely be described as empty space, and not the kind one might expect to become a stage, either theatrical or national. As I drove there, I stopped a couple of times on the side of the road to take photos of the vistas, just miles and miles of landscape. The openness of the space was enough to prompt anxiety—the prospect of being alone and abandoned in that space. Of course, the space isn't really historyless, with the legacies of a violent settler colonialism dotting the trip. But even the most carefully chosen vistas weren't empty. Every photo I took was intersected by fences, a truly dizzying variety when I reviewed them: from old-timey split-rail fences to electrified wire fences to larger and more imposing metal structures with difficult-to-intuit placements and purposes.

I didn't try to visit the fence where Shepard was discovered. The road names have changed, the thing is on private property, and I wasn't making a pilgrimage in any particular way. But I did think, standing along the side of the road in Southern Wyoming, feeling a little panicky about the mere thought of the loneliness proposed by that landscape, how much more horrific it would be along any one of those fences, knowing I was going to die.

When I arrived at the University of Wyoming campus, I went to see the only memorial that was established in Laramie, a memorial bench with a plaque:

MATTHEW WAYNE SHEPARD
DECEMBER 1, 1976 - OCTOBER 12, 1998
BELOVED SON, BROTHER, AND FRIEND
HE CONTINUES TO MAKE A DIFFERENCE
PEACE BE WITH HIM AND ALL WHO SIT HERE

The bench was dedicated in 2008, ten years after Shepard's death. Even the National Park Service, in a listing of LGBTQ Memorials, notes, "some critics argue that the memorial bench should be more explicit about who Matthew Shepard was and why he was killed. To many, the Matthew Shepard Memorial is understated, and because it took ten years to erect, long overdue."[32] The day I visited, the bench remained decorated with a deflated balloon, a few bunches of dried roses, and a couple of makeshift shrines of stones and pinecones on the seat that made sitting actually difficult. Perhaps because of the pandemic, the now-dead flowers and now-deflated balloon had not been removed. The bench was one of several on Quealy Plaza, dedicated to former University of Wyoming trustee Patrick J. Quealy Jr., scion of a Wyoming mining interest. Quealy passed away just a year before Shepard, but the plaza was completed in 2001. The disparity is telling. Another bench around the corner memorialized the dead mother of a former president of the university. About a hundred feet away, a large statue of Benjamin Franklin stood, commemorating the statesman's 250th birthday in 1956, though the connection to Wyoming remains somewhat mysterious. The politics of commemoration in this spot are fraught to say the least. The vision of the future they enact is even less clear. What is the history that Quealy Plaza asks us to remember? The utopia it asks us to glimpse?

Instead: a disappointing reality, twenty years after the hopefulness of *The Laramie Project*. One might hope for a town still enlivened by the public deliberation that its most prominent tragedy engendered. However, it is important to remember that the conversation performed on stages across America—it was for a time one of the most performed plays in the US—may have been drawn entirely from words spoken by the residents of Laramie; but the public sphere represented is itself a fabrication, a collage of thoughts, ideas, and utterances often spoken in private moments, but never fully entered into a broad public debate.[33] In fact, it is difficult to imagine such a deliberative conversation happening organically in any real place. In this way, while so many elements of this "theater of the real" are grounded in history—in a verifiable past—and while so much of that verifiable past fuels these plays' politics of pluralist deliberation, we must see that the utopian public sphere they weave together is precisely the fiction that doesn't yet exist. And though I hold on to "yet," we also know that debates about Matthew Shepard are part of history—this play (like *Guantanamo* staged in DC after the release of the Tipton Three) could only ever be about the present of deliberation and its recent past. Perhaps then, these "utopias" were never oriented toward futurity, but merely toward enabling a smoothly functioning public sphere in the present. And further, we come to understand the very impossibility of this idealized public sphere happening "in the wild," as it were, and we may conclude that in order to experience rational public deliberation, *it had to be staged.*

• • •

And what kind of utopias are we wishing for anyway? A world in which the inhumane torture of other people isn't predicated on dragnets of faith and ethnicity (dare we hope for a world where torture doesn't happen at all)? A place where young men are not murdered for desiring other young men? These are hardly the queer theres and thens imagined—even glimpsed—by José Esteban Muñoz, as "the warm illumination of a horizon imbued with possibility . . . an ideality that can be distilled from the past and used to imagine a future . . . [and] an educated mode of desiring that allows us to see and feel beyond the quagmire of the present."[34] Muñoz's writing offers a frame for utopia as a concrete future of potentiality, extending well beyond what *The Laramie Project* or *Guanatanamo* suggests that we might envision. Even Jill Dolan's wish for utopia in Laramie is modest enough—a world in which theater can "claim its place as a vital part of the public sphere," relational in its hope for the future. But it's also not much of "an ideality . . . distilled from [this particular] past," and it is hardly the queerly utopian future that Muñoz envisions.[35]

Dolan, elsewhere in her book, is certainly capable of finding more radical versions of hope in the theater. The limitation, I'd argue, is not Dolan's but *Laramie*'s—a project that limits its utopianism to something more like what Lauren Berlant describes as "the desire for the political"—expressed neatly nonetheless in Dolan's fervent wishes for a theatrical public sphere. The desire for the political for Berlant figures prominently in these performances, and, indeed, may be a uniting feature of verbatim plays that engage the idea that the future change promised by the form is a more livable world for both their speakers and their audiences. Berlant defines this desire in several ways, noting first that "intensely political seasons [the sort, perhaps, that prompt verbatim theater performances] spawn reveries of a different immediacy. People imagine alternative environments where authenticity trumps ideology, truths cannot be concealed, and communication feels intimate, face-to-face," what amounts to, essentially, "a post-public sphere public," and later, "the desire for alternative filters that produce the sense—if not the scene—of a more livable and intimate sociality."[36] This desire, Berlant argues, reveals itself not in traditional public spheres, but more intimate ones, where "one senses that matters of survival are at stake and that collective mediation through narration and audition might provide some routes out of the impasses and the struggle of the present, or at least some sense that there would be recognition that the participants were in the room together;" where "minimally, you just need to perform audition to listen and to be interested in the scene's visceral impact;" and where "each person can contribute . . . a personal story about not being defeated by what is overwhelming."[37]

The hope that we might find at the theater (to use Dolan's phrase), then, is a hope that the public sphere might model this more intimate public, where "each person can contribute"—everyone from the Laramie sheriff to the town's Baptist minister, to a Muslim college student, from the US Secretary of Defense to a detainee in a US prison camp. This more intimate public contrasts starkly with the "live and let live" motto re-hashed by so many Laramie narrators. Perhaps audience members do not typically contribute in such an intimate theatrical public (though post-show discussions and other dramaturged activities might intervene); yet it is the site for precisely the kind of utopian intersubjectivity that, elsewhere in her study, Dolan locates most palpably in theatrical performance. Here, the being-in-the-room-togetherness of theater is imagined as creating a kind of affect world that is, if not directly political, then what Berlant calls "juxtapolitical." The utopian thinking of such performances becomes a political world in which one might make their way, but I would argue is precisely the desire that is enabled and enacted by these performances' desire for change and their belief that they ritualize a public-sphere engagement that works toward that change.

The open question, then, is whether this utopianism bears fruit, or whether over the past several decades, it has simply reproduced the conditions of exclusion. Has all of this discussion (to return to Raymond Geuss) only succeeded in fetishizing discussion itself? Has the process only opened a wedge into our political discourse by which—today!—fascism, homophobic hate, white supremacy, and all other matters of anti-sociality might be re-admitted? Berlant might call this phenomenon a "relation of cruel optimism," then, where "the object/scene of desire is itself an obstacle to fulfilling the very wants that bring people to it . . . when, despite an awareness that the normative political sphere appears as a shrunken, broken, or distant place of activity among elites, members of the body politic return periodically to its recommitment ceremonies and scenes."[38] And so, these performances teeter on the precipice of a fetishistic attachment to a political process of engaged deliberation that has and will continue to disenfranchise its own speakers, or alternatively, an affective mode of being-otherwise that allows the narrators and auditors of this more intimate (theatrical) public to imagine and potentially enact ways of surviving by simply being in the room together. To Berlant, "the compulsion to repeat a toxic optimism can suture someone or a world to a cramped and unimaginative space of committed replication, *just in case* it will be different."[39]

The utopian peg on which verbatim theater has hung its hopes, then, is the tethering of the political to the affective—to deliberating and feeling together in the phenomenal space of the theater. And whether this optimism is toxic or transformative depends upon its ability "to reinvent," as Berlant notes, "new idioms of the political, and of belonging itself."[40] That is to say, even inasmuch as any public sphere might be an affect world, verbatim theatrical performances (particularly in the neoliberal period preceding our recent lurch to the right) have sought to seal intimacy (if that's what they even seek), not just with rational deliberation, but with *feeling together*: with empathy.

3 Feeling Together

We hear about empathy a great deal in public discourse, especially liberal public discourse. We hear about empathy a lot in the theater, especially. As a concept, empathy has come to bear a great deal of weight as a mechanism for a heterogenous society, the ethical lubricant for living together in a cosmopolitan, multicultural, and fractious democracy. But as much as public discourse may depend on empathy, we struggle to define it. Depending on whom you ask, empathy could be ethical, social, historically contingent, rhetorical, cognitive, embodied (even kinesthetic), and/or political. While there exists tension among these many definitions, I will work with a simple and broad one that follows Suzanne Keen—"the vicarious, spontaneous sharing of affect"—that will expand over the course of this chapter across several of these dimensions.[1] In short, though: empathy is a feeling-together, as opposed to the feeling-for of sympathy, and supplemental to the thinking-together that tends to inhere in discourses of a rational public sphere.

Feeling together. Within this comparatively simple concept, we might come to understand how acting as an artform employs and potentially models the processes of empathetically taking on the perspective of another; how empathy drives the ethical engagement with others (and Others); how empathy connects emotional feelings to the physical mirroring of another body in space; how empathy functions in the psychology of an individual, serves that individual in society, and simultaneously operates as an effect of neurological structures; how our understanding of the concept of empathy has shifted over the past century or so, coming to be seen particularly (but by no means only) as a remedy to racism across the same period that this study covers. We might view empathy, too, as an affective structure along which the political life of emotion is conducted and across which rhetorical effects might be crafted and deployed.

In the context of verbatim theater (and in particular, existing scholarship on verbatim theater), empathy is deeply embedded in the process of listening: not simply the audience listening to a performance, but more importantly, the listening that happens when the performer listens to the person whose words are reperformed on the stage. In this formulation, empathy for another, first and foremost, *depends* on listening. Robin Bernstein's early work on Anna Deavere Smith declares that "Smith's work required empathy for all her characters," while Gregory Jay argues that "Smith intends audiences and readers to engage in the same labor of unsettling cross-cultural empathy with loss that she herself performs on stage."[2] And Smith herself narrates the initiating moments of her whole artistic project in the question, "If I were to go around and listen listen listen to Americans, would I end up with some kind of composite that would tell me more than what is *evidently* there?"[3] Della Pollock insists that multiplicities of oral history performance "democratizes tellers and listeners by easing the monologic power of *what is said* into the collaborative, cogenerative, and yet potentially discordant *act of saying and hearing it*."[4] And while Pollock is cautionary about empathy as potentially mystifying, her insistence on listening-as-democratic and others' insistence on listening-as-empathetic offers a kind of fulcrum for thinking through listening as a key mechanism for an empathetic public sphere. Berlant sees this in the intimate publics where "you just need to *perform audition*, to listen and be interested in the scene's visceral impact."[5] But as much as Pollock insists on the "'response-ability' of the person who hears oral histories and the corresponding strength of that person's agency as someone who acts on hearing if only by telling again," others might critique the potential of that listening, of performing audition, to be fundamentally passive when urgent social action is needed.[6]

• • •

I am, so I think, a pretty empathetic person. Writing this chapter during the middle of the COVID-19 pandemic has posed particular challenges and opportunities for me. Like many of the readers of this sentence, I cried at least weekly through much of 2020. My anxieties were high and my motivation was low, despite the fact that my situation was privileged and comfortable. My affinity for empathy, perhaps even my overt valorization of empathy, nonetheless helped me stay alert to the experiences of colleagues and friends who had lost a loved one, or who were scared, or who felt very alone. I do not describe this as a particular virtue, per se, because I certainly didn't do anything especially noteworthy in the face of this weeping on behalf of people on social media, or in response to news stories. Tenderness (one kind of precursor to empathy) in my case yielded no particularly concrete outcomes during the long months of the pandemic (and my children, trapped in the house with me, may remark that my emotional vulnerabilities to others made me perhaps less tender with them). Nonetheless, I have been carrying this value with me, and accordingly, I tend to believe that my openness to empathetic response has made me, therefore, more open to social justice movements and scholarship, when (as a cis-het white man from the middle class), it might have been more obvious to stay out of the fray (to the degree that I am *in* the fray). At the least, an empathetic set of responses helped me remain as open as I could to the resurgence of the #BlackLivesMatter movement in the summer of 2020, and drove the small actions that I took on in that context.

This is a rosy self-vision, though, and as an empathetic optimist prone to utopian thinking, I have come to understand how this self-conception has facilitated an aesthetic-political gravitation toward the bridge-building impulses of the performances that this book describes. You can perhaps imagine my response, then, to the final episode of the spring 2019 season of the podcast *Invisibilia* entitled, provocatively, "The End of Empathy."[7] In this episode, the decidedly Gen-X feminist hosts of the podcast, Hanna Rosin and Alix Spiegel, introduced the reporting of their guest producer, the avowedly millennial Lina Misitzis, acknowledging that their own upbringing in the '70's had forged the empathetic ethos of their show that Misitzis was about to challenge:

> ROSIN: In my elementary school in the '70s, which wasn't progressive or mushy in any way, we wrote letters to pretend Russian pen pals to teach us to open our hearts to our enemies; and not just enemies—also people who were suffering. Some civil rights activists were really big on empathy. People with power and privilege were supposed to open their hearts to the realities of people without power, not from the safe, noblesse oblige distance of pity but from the inside. That's what I learned about how you make the world better.[8]

Rosin and Spiegel handed over the reins as part of a job interview exercise, passing along the tapes of an interview and asking applicants to make a story out of it. They tapped Misitzis, because, as they put it:

> The story we got back from Lina was so not what we expected—almost the opposite of what we created—that it felt for us like a moment of reckoning. See, Lina's description of our show is right. The INVISIBILIA way is the empathic way. But Lina—and really much of the world—seems to be losing patience with that way. In the post-#MeToo, vigilant, polarized Trump-era world, showing empathy for your so-called enemies is practically taboo.[9]

The conclusions they reach, looking at contemporary media as well as some emerging social science, is that empathy has its political limits, in part because empathy functions best when we already share affinities with those we might empathize with, making dialogue across difference more difficult (quite counter to prevailing discourse).[10] The episode concluded on a note that required Rosin to acknowledge that the empathetic impulse had caused her to "fundamentally misread the person I was supposed to be empathizing with."[11] While the next chapter will discuss the stance of suspicion that characterized Misitzis's approach to that story, I was first most interested in what I understood as a generational affinity with Rosin and Spiegel, an historically situated and politically undergirded valuing of empathy as a world-righting activity. I also noted, as they did, that the historical situation and the political landscape had shifted.

First, then: empathy is historical. While generational stereotyping doesn't make for great cultural criticism (does it matter that Barack Obama is a late Baby Boomer, rather than an early Gen-Xer?), historicizing a common context of Cold-war politics and the triumph of neoliberal capitalism over communism does. And in precisely this context we see the historical contingency of co-feeling as a moral and political imperative. I find no random coincidence in the height of empathy-driven verbatim performance and (for example) the eight-year presidency of Bill Clinton, who campaigned on the centrist Third Way, a particularly neoliberal form of Democratic party politics that emphasized entrepreneurship, globalization, and softly liberal social policy. During that first campaign, Clinton famously said to a protester, "I feel your pain."[12] Similarly, at the end of this period, George W. Bush ticked the empathy box (albeit somewhat tenuously) by running on a platform of "compassionate conservatism." These two politicians, both so directly affiliated (even across political parties) with economic policies and public personas that combined politics of neoliberalism with an interpersonal appeal ("He feels my pain!" "I'd have a beer with him!"), together define the pinnacle of a particular moment that also contains within it a third key principle: liberal pluralism. Carolyn Pedwell, writing about the double-edged use of empathy in the Obama era, extends this history closer to the present, noting both neoliberal continuities in this jaundiced deployment of empathy, but also important distinctions, drawn from feminist and anti-racist stances, in terms like "'mutuality,' 'debt,' and 'obligation.'" This ambivalent negotiation shows up palpably in the verbatim theater that emerged in the first decade of the new millennium.

But these discourses have longer histories, too. When historian Susan Lanzoni, in her history of the concept of empathy from its first appearances in the new science of psychology to the cognitive science of today, turns to politics in the 1960s and '70s, it is not to reference the Cold War as Hanna Rosin did, but rather to frame it as a key intervention in the politics of civil rights. She follows the career of eminent social psychologist Kenneth B. Clark, whose work on African American urban populations clearly linked the future success of social movements to the cultivation of empathetic reasoning. This capacity related directly to the exercise of power, as Lanzoni writes, "Clark had indeed pitted power against empathy: the powerful in society clearly lacked this ability, or they would not structure and support the kinds of brutal inequalities that continued to exist in American society."[13] Even though her chapter on "Empathy, Race, and Politics" ends in the early 1980s (just when Anna Deavere Smith was beginning her "search for American character,") Lanzoni notes that others see "empathy as critical to social justice, human rights, and even the procedures of deliberative democracy," while "others support empathy's political importance but warn against a neo-liberal, market-oriented vision of empathy which judges it as just another skill to be developed by the self-enterprising."[14] In closing her chapter, she wonders about the political potential of empathy by noting that "empathy, by itself, may not be enough."[15]

But for some period that began before the rise of Paul Volcker's economic policies, and persisted at least up to the cataclysm of 9/11/2001, empathy seemed a crucial component of moral politics, underpinning a multicultural vision in which people with many different identities might live alongside one another in a way that valued difference, thrived because of it, made personal value out of it, and resolved conflict by talking through it.

David Savran, writing about *Angels in America*'s liberal pluralist social vision of utopia, notes that the play's simultaneous ability to generate economic and cultural capital alongside its politics of difference represents something of a bourgeois liberal ambivalence, one that argues for equality while domesticating dissent. Savran is tempted to "see the celebrity of *Angels in America* as yet another measure of the power of liberal pluralism to neutralize oppositional practices."[16] The same ambivalence that Savran finds in *Angels* might just as easily be found in *Fires in the Mirror*, *The Laramie Project*, and even war-on-terror verbatim plays like Robin Soans's *Talking to Terrorists*. Certainly, these plays suggest a kind of democratic deliberation through both de-hierarchized, pluralist speaking, as well as empathetic listening across difference; they might also be said to "neutralize oppositional practices" simply by suggesting that representation itself is a remedy—even as these plays have generated economic and cultural capital for the artists and any number of other cultural producers (theater and publishing professionals alike). In this context, liberal pluralism, spectacularized through displays of empathy, could then become a kind of ethno-social fantasy that would underpin neoliberalism's national and transnational fantasies of diverse representation as a *substitute for* rather than a *step toward* equity and justice.

• • •

And so even as empathy may be historical, it is therefore also unavoidably political. As much as remembering together and feeling together are enabled through empathetic listening, and as much as empathetic listening may or may not enable social change, we can largely understand this impulse toward the social good of empathetic listening as offering a specific remedy to the cultural effects of a pervasive neoliberal political economy. Insofar as neoliberalism might be said to have cultural effects, those effects might be identified (as many have noted) as the commodification of otherwise noncommercial components of daily life, of the restructuring of meaningful interpersonal relationships as potentially or even primarily economic ones, of an increasing isolation of care to individuals and ever-smaller heteronormative family units, and of a valorization of competition as a primary social organizing tool. We have seen these effects dramatically exacerbated during the experience of the COVID-19 pandemic, where concerns of public and personal health have come into sharp conflict with demands for economic solvency. This played out not just in debates about whether, how, and how much to "open the economy" versus applying business restrictions to stem virus transmission, but also in the race to profit from the "new normal" on the backs of underpaid and disproportionately brown and black workers; in the lonelinesses of pandemic isolation for single adults and empty-nesters; in the politics of educational pods and university teaching modalities; in the allocation of the earliest experimental COVID-19 treatments for the wealthy and powerful; and in debates about who "deserves" vaccine priority, sometimes revolving around the "accountability" of life behaviors that correlate with comorbidity factors like obesity, smoking, and alcoholism.

Pedwell notes that discourses of empathy in the cultural moment leading up to the Obama era and beyond, hinge on two contradictory political frameworks: on one hand, Pedwell points to the proliferation of feminist and anti-racist calls for empathy across empowerments to remedy global and gendered inequities. Citing critical luminaries like Martha Nussbaum, Sara Ahmed, Chandra Talpade Mohanty, and Lauren Berlant, Pedwell teases out the global political dimensions of empathy as an affect that demands perspective-taking as a precondition for the reciprocity needed for social change. But in contrast to this approach, Pedwell also locates in this framework precisely the neoliberal valuation of empathy as a crucial business skill, one that can be leveraged to pry open global markets for greater economic penetration. In this context, Pedwell argues, "empathy is understood as a technology for 'creating the many', a means to maximize economic competitiveness and growth within transnational circuits of capital."[17] In this way, empathy is not just a skill or tool for creating economic value, it is an economy itself, and like all affective economies (following Ahmed), the empathy economy can be deployed in a range of ideological directions, perhaps toward encouraging mutual obligation to Others (as social theorists like Nussbaum and Mohanty argue), perhaps toward mobilizing fear against "terrorists" (as Ahmed details), and perhaps toward erasing the public offense of sexist abusers (as podcaster Misitzis identifies).[18] In this way, empathy functions neither as an ideology nor as an emotion itself, but rather as a flexible structure along which emotion (and with it, power and capital) might circulate.[19]

While Pedwell identifies the nuanced ways that these competing discourses of empathy operate in the context of neoliberalism, we must further identify them both as specifically *symptomatic of* neoliberalism. That is to say, if feminist and anti-racist activists persistently identify empathy as a way to address the calloused exploitation and oppression of those marginalized from the centers of power, we might simultaneously recognize that empathy is touted in this line of argument particularly because emotion seems to be freighted with the power to escape commodification and to ameliorate the dehumanizing effects of the persistent application of market logics to human experience. If those in power could simply take on the perspective of those people who are daily ground down by the exigencies of global neoliberalism, the reasoning goes, they might be less inclined to support that framework with such vigor. Transnational women's movements, for example, might find greater solidarity and, therefore, more resistant power by first establishing common ground through common feeling. By this logic, common feeling might be a pathway for power that explicitly denies marketization: emotional mutuality as a brake on human commodification then is *absolutely* symptomatic of the relentless advance of commodification on every aspect of human experience under the regime of global neoliberalism. And just as empathy is symptomatic as a *response* to human commodification, we must then not be surprised by Pedwell's identification of the fact that, inexorably, empathy has itself become commodified as a tool for further market reach into the human psyche.

Verbatim theater has not been immune from this specifically neoliberal deployment of empathy for marketing purposes. As Lisa Aikman notes, "In 2007, representatives of Unilever approached the prolific and internationally-produced Canadian playwright Judith Thompson to ask if she would be interested in writing a play about beauty and aging, using 'real women' over the age of 45 as performers as part of the Dove Campaign for Real Beauty."[20] The resulting play, 2007's *Body and Soul*, is an exercise in both empathy and (unsurprising for a playwright of Thompson's force) feminist power. But, as Sorouja Moll notes, "Thompson's unscripted ways of operating, even under corporate pressure, incited the interruption of the corporate strategies of 'beauty' and the 'real' with *jubilant* and *warlike* discoveries: a method of discovery and dissent that happened from within."[21] Moll characterizes the play as a negotiation, one that Thompson and collaborators eventually walked away from, producing the play outside of the auspices of the Dove marketing campaign. Aikman notes in particular the playwright's deployment of empathy in the process of creating the play, as a subject who herself was one of the demographic group represented in the play. Reading the play as a deployment of feminist tactics of affirmation within and against Unilever's strategic gambit to "demonstrate that beauty has no age limit" as part of a broader "hope . . . that women will like what Dove is doing and will support Dove so we can continue to do this kind of great work," Moll underscores the multivalent and even contested functioning of empathy within this neoliberal context.[22]

The attempted and ambivalent cooptation of empathy from ultra-humane-framework-for-resistance-to-neoliberal-dehumanization to tool-for-expanding-the-global-reach-of-market-logics may feel queasily predictable, but also underscores the notion that empathy is, itself, ideologically flexible. Even so, empathy functions in both of these configurations as a classically *liberal* responses to our neoliberal moment, because that response presumes specifically bourgeois-liberal preconditions (the individual as a self-determining subject within frameworks of economic and political participation) for advancing the totalizing logic of commodified selfhood (the valuation of the individual specifically within a framework of economic exchange). So, even if empathetic listening, perspective-taking, and co-feeling might be mechanisms to preserve a kind of resistant human thriving in the face of the pervasive marketization of human experience, these mechanisms depend on an understanding of the subject as already inside liberal culture. To clarify: if we understand the idea of taking on one another's perspectives as a technique to achieve better governance and a more just society, we have to realize that our current social precondition is self-interest rather than mutuality. If an obligation to one another requires a secondary mechanism (say, empathy) in order to connect individuals, we might see in this a signal that the individual selfhood of the enlightenment subject—all the way back to Descartes's *cogito, ergo sum*—is still the organizing unit of political society, and that collective understandings of social organization have to be imagined anew from the starting point of the individual social/economic subject. There's no room in this model, then, to understand subjectivity as already collective, or even in any significant way plural.

• • •

I recognize that this project teeters on a palpable ambivalence, this emerging understanding that verbatim theater's dependence on represented dialogue and the affective dimensions of listening are a particularly bourgeois-liberal response to the encroachment of neoliberal political economy on our feeling lives, and the simultaneous belief (which I am not entirely willing to abandon), that the affective dimensions of listening are a crucial and oft-missing component of our current political discourse. I recognize too that my own desire for the political in the theater is for a space for listening. I do still want to come to the theater to hear from Others whom I may not meet in my daily life, to hear from those who have not yet had a seat at my table, to hear from those who have often been silenced. This desire appears in a way that is explicitly denied and ridiculed (charges of "snowflake!" are never more than a tweet away) by a far-right politics that lurches—even lunges—toward authoritarianism. At the same time, this desire might also be regarded as passive and ineffectual, as an obstacle to direct action, and even as complicit in maintaining the status quo that keeps Others outside the actual decision-making part of public and political life, the *democracy* of democratic deliberation. Even as the verbatim performances of anglophone western democracies have sought to bring more people into the deliberative spaces that we show on-stage, do our utopian visions of an empathetic public sphere sop up the anger that might drive us to actual better ways of being?

Pedwell, too, is careful to note that "while empathy is envisioned as an affective catalyst for radical self-transformation which can lead to social action, theorists argue that empathy is, more often than not, rather passive or fleeting."[23] She cites, among other theorists, Berlant's concern about "the centrality of economies of suffering to mass capitalist aesthetics" and the ways that "specific kinds of collective but individually experienced pain get turned into modern forms of entertainment."[24] We will be forced to ask these questions about, for example, devised pieces that stage the narratives of marginalized voices, perhaps most palpably in performances like Ping Chong's 2002 *Children of War* or Soans's *Talking to Terrorists*. Passivity is perhaps a greater concern; even as Pedwell cites Ahmed's argument that empathy's outcomes are always unknowable, Jodi Dean voices the concern that deliberative democracy is all discussion and no action, which identifies real gaps in the value of empathy to political transformation. "Democracy seems limited to the discussions surrounding a decision, the discursive context of a decision, but forever unable to reach the decision itself," Dean writes. "The decision continues to exceed the circulation of reasons."[25] If deliberation is itself often posed as an end in and of itself, an infinite deferral of political action in favor of political good-feeling (and good feeling together), then verbatim theater's modeling of an empathic public sphere for precisely this kind of democratic deliberation will almost necessarily trend in the direction of deferred action that Dean bemoans as "unable to elaborate a convincing political alternative because it accepts the premise that we already know what is to be done—critique, discuss, include, and revise."[26]

I am left wondering: Can we imagine a theater that remedies the refusal to listen (and worse: the refusal to care) of this rightward lurch, without clogging up the workings of direct action for social change? What if this theater is no longer a verbatim theater? What if it never was? What if (I feel compelled to ask) it might still be?

• • •

This current apparent crisis does point the way to imagining other models. What if, instead of a Habermasian public sphere, we imagined a Levinasian one? That is to say, if empathy signifies the traversing the space between self and other, we might benefit from a public sphere that negotiates this space, not with rational debate, but with the kind of face-to-face encounter that French philosopher Emmanuel Levinas identifies as the irreducible site of ethics, where we are called into an obligation to take responsibility to care for the Other we meet in this encounter. How, following this obligation, would we conceive of a model of public deliberation that imagines itself not as a space in which equally competent deliberators engage in even-handed democratic deliberation, but, instead, as one composed of human faces that say to one another: *love me* and *do not destroy me*? What if the problem that we mull over is not the issue we discuss but the ways that we listen, particularly across difference?

Admittedly, Levinas's work sits somewhat uneasily with both discussions of the Habermasian public sphere and discussions of empathy. Habermas and Levinas are largely regarded as incommensurable precisely because the public sphere (in Habermas's conception) emerged as a space in which to resolve private dispute based on rational public discourse, a kind of exchange already imagined as oppositional to Levinas's dictum to respect the radical Otherness of other subjects without reducing or demeaning them (indeed, this irreducible Otherness is also an obstacle to imagining the "feeling-together" of empathy as an ethical act). Educational theorist Guoping Zhao nonetheless seeks to reconcile these ways of approaching public discourse, considering Levinas as a corrective to Habermas's general inability to account for difference among participants in the rational public sphere. Reading Levinas closely, Zhao maintains that "to preserve the alterity and subjectivity of the other, the only ways of expression and communication are through responsibility and discourse."[27] If we then imagine a public sphere predicated on respecting difference, and deliberating over the common good with that respect for difference as not only a precondition but an inviolable norm, then "the public sphere where a speech act is carried out can indeed be made into the space where subjectivity and otherness can be maintained, and intersubjective human responsibility can be nurtured."[28]

Seyla Benhabib similarly finds pre-existing conceptions of the public sphere insufficient to the moment, but nonetheless outlines how a diverse society might re-envision itself:

> To recognize and to come to grips with the implications of its own diversity, a democratic people needs to reenact its identity in the public sphere. . . . This process of self-representation and articulation in public is still the only means through which the *civic imagination* can be cultivated. The process of articulating good reasons in public forces one to take the standpoint of all others to whom one is trying to make one's point of view plausible and cogent, and to whom one is trying to tell one's own story. The ability of individuals and groups to take the standpoint of others into account, to be able to reverse perspectives and see the world from their point of view, is a crucial virtue of moral and aesthetic imagination in a civic polity. Certainly this ability becomes most necessary as well as most fragile under conditions of incommensurability and social opacity.[29]

Benhabib's vision for a new public sphere was articulated in the Clinton years—sometime between *Twilight: Los Angeles, 1992* and *The Laramie Project*—and while its argument nonetheless depends upon "trying to make one's point of view plausible and cogent" rather than "intimately felt," hers is a theory of civic imagination that tends toward empathetic listening in much the same way that documentary theater of that moment sought to enact.

This is to say: the utopian vision of a theatricalized public sphere has tended to rely upon the infusion of empathy into modes of discourse. Hinging upon an understanding of the centrality, not just of the voices represented on stage but the implied dramaturgical act of engaged listening, these performances seek not just to model the deliberations of an imagined functioning public, but to model the ways of being in those deliberations. Here though, instead of focusing on the rational, the competent, the rhetorically savvy, we find a mode of public deliberation that depends on the feeling-together modes of empathetic listening. Verbatim theater's utopia, then, is not a stage for arguing-at, but a space for feeling-with.

That is not to say that empathy-producing storytelling on stage doesn't itself have a rhetorical function. In the most simplistic iteration, we need look no further than the Aristotelian tradition to see this in action. The appeal to pathos may seek empathetic connection, though as Lisa Blankenship notes, the Aristotelian tradition tends to foreground a strategic surface engagement designed to defeat an opponent in a contest of rhetorical prowess that foregrounds resolving dissensus through effectively advancing one's own position, rather than finding consensus through deep and responsive listening.[30] She advances as an alternative the idea of "rhetorical empathy," wherein "approaching others in rhetorical engagements must begin with changing ourselves, with listening, with trying to understand the personal and political factors that influence the person who makes our blood boil."[31] One component of this idea, of moving past surface engagements with others and opening up our rhetorical selves to really hearing those with whom we engage, involves "*staging empathy*—performing empathy even though at the initial stages [a speaker] might be resistant to [others] views" in order to "move toward *deep empathy*."[32] This process, not surprisingly, is one that Blankenship connects to Levinas's emphasis on bodies "interacting with one another, an exposedness, a vulnerability, and an 'obligation to respond' that forms the basis for all ethics."[33] This notion of *staging empathy* as a movement toward *deep empathy* does not deny that there is strategic value in that cultivation of empathy, but insists that it can and must be enacted from a place that prioritizes difference, engages it through listening before speaking, and opens up all parties to being changed by the process.

A theatrical process that prioritizes rhetorical empathy might be seen as central to an idealized public sphere that operates through empathy and through an affective engagement with others. To be sure, to imagine much verbatim theater of this period in this way aligns neatly with the ways that many practitioners and scholars have discussed the form. At the same time, that process is (like all conceptions of empathy in the neoliberal era) open for more cynical deployments of pointedly combative rhetoric, and then in some cases, ambivalent productions that oscillate between genuine attempts at a rhetoric of empathy and stances shot through with presumed enmity. To be sure the political theater staged during the eight neoconservative years of the George W. Bush administration—which saw an especially thorough advance of neoliberal cultural values—offer palpable illustrations of the contested and ambivalent entanglements of empathy on western democracies' liberal-political stages. In 2008, David Edgar identified that particular resurgence of the form as especially pointed and especially political, particularly in the UK tradition of the tribunal play as a response to the so-called "war on terror."

I have written about these plays before—Soans's *Talking to Terrorists*, David Hare's *Stuff Happens*, and Victoria Brittain and Gillian Slovo's *Guantanamo: 'Honor Bound to Defend Freedom'*—noting a decade ago that those plays' failures to listen empathetically was conditioned by their specifically western political frameworks. And certainly, 9/11 and its aftermath—the Islamophobia, the USA PATRIOT Act, the hunger for war—revealed the limits of western democracy's yearning for empathy as a political engine, for even these plays (which I think of as operating in a distinctly different stage of verbatim theater's development) struggle to balance listening with an antagonistic stance. Antagonistic *to whom* was less clear to me: actual terrorists? War-hawk politicians? Complicit voters? And while those plays' faith in empathy wavered, mine did not: "That Soans's play takes its title from a strategy to defeat its subjects tells us much about its own political aims," I wrote. "Talking *to* Others, or *about* Others may not represent any particular promise. But listening to them just might."[34]

Encountering difference continues to figure prominently in these discussions. Just as Lanzoni identifies empathy's emergence from conversations about psychology into political discourse through the context of civil rights and discussions of racial difference, we saw empathy's continued deployment in the new century as a mechanism to make sense of other kinds of difference as well. Andreea Deciu Ritivoi, writing about the narrativization of empathy in the stories of Syrian refugee children, notes that "difference is a major obstacle to empathic understanding, but it is also an inevitable feature of intersubjectivity."[35] Her argument hinges on the power of stories to enable an empathetic public sphere:

> If narratives can trigger empathic responses, they could be used to promote a compassionate politics that encourages us to understand extreme experiences that we might have not had the misfortune to encounter. Narratives draw us toward other subjectivities, not merely to observe and examine them but to make sense of them and to look at the world from within their perspectives.[36]

Ritivoi suggests that narratives have a specific rhetorical pull, that they function to insert a particularly potent pathos into spaces in which providing reasons might otherwise dominate. She identifies Hans-Georg Gadamer's notion of intersubjectivity—a notion also powerfully deployed by Jill Dolan in her explication of utopian performatives—to develop a theory of narrative empathy that does not hinge on pre-identified commonalities beyond the narrative itself, but rather depends upon the focalization of perspective in narrative to expand, in Gadamer's terms, the horizons of experience itself.

Ritivoi, then, poses a theory of narrative empathy, like Blankenship's theory of rhetorical empathy, that is predicated upon an openness to being affected by narratives of the Other whose very difference might move us to action. Her central example is an appeal from the United Nations High Commissioner for Refugees (UNHCR) which focuses its persuasive energy on the narrative of three-year-old Ashraf, a child whose whole life has taken place during the Syrian conflict. She identifies ways that, despite sharing little in common with those to whom the appeal is directed, Ashraf has experienced a concrete set of lived details that allow readers to make the "epistemic leap" to understanding the general experience of Syrian refugees in crisis. "Such a dialectic of general and particular, new and familiar, difference and sameness," Ritivoi writes, "defines the parameters for empathy as the product of a situated understanding uniquely tied to narrative."[37] And indeed, while Ritivoi asserts the rhetorical potential of empathetic narrative through the story of a refugee child, we must understand the potentially amplified power of such narratives when embodied in performance.

This empathetic power might be even more powerfully deployed when embodied by the children themselves, as is the case in Ping Chong's *Children of War*. While many verbatim performances move from the listening space of the oral history into a performance by an actor who may or may not have participated in those interviews, Ping Chong's method, deployed across the many performances of the *Undesirable Elements* series, involved devising a script based on discussions with several interview subjects and then handing that script back to those non-professional speakers to perform themselves for an audience. Theatrically quite static, but nonetheless profoundly affecting, performances from this series cultivate a particularly potent form of rhetorical empathy by presenting the particular narratives of people who have suffered specific human indignities and injustices marked by a common theme or identity; connecting them to one another to draw a generalized portrait of that injustice; and presenting them with the powerful authenticity effect of the real people themselves, telling their own stories together, live in performance. *Children of War*, initially presented in

2002 just outside of Washington, DC, featured six performers—some still teenagers—who lived locally but had emigrated to the US as children seeking refuge from violence in El Salvador, Kurdistan, Iran, Afghanistan, and Sierra Leone.[38]

Children of War gives audiences stories, sometimes collectively narrated, sometimes individually told, that detail risk, fear, violence, loss, defiance, and then—upon arrival in the US—some mixture of hopefulness and resilience alongside the continued indignities of racism and xenophobia. While each story is particular to the performer/narrator (some of whom were still in childhood when the play was performed), general threads of common kinds of experience emerge, allowing audiences to (as Ritivoi suggests) devise a generalized picture of refugee experience. Sometimes these have an explicitly affective component (stories of murdered loved ones and bombed homes evoke deep pathos). Others are more pointedly political, and implicitly rhetorical. For example, the European colonial roots of many current conflicts are woven into the narrative from the beginning in a way that implicates the presumably predominantly white audiences at Theater of the First Amendment (TFA) in suburban Fairfax, Virginia. Fatu's story begins in 1492 with the Portuguese explorer who first put "Serra Lyoa" on a European map, while Dereen's story features the 1921 division of Kurdistan among British and French interests.[39] Similarly, Yarvin tells of offensive remarks made about her not learning English, Dereen tells of being accused of being a Saddam Hussein sympathizer, and Abdul relates a story of not being believed by classmates to whom he had told parts of his past.[40] Ping Chong's strategically constructed script deploys stories that invite the audience to make affective connections with the speakers in front of them as part of a deliberation over the implicit question, "How should we receive refugees into our communities?" In short, *Children of War* "stages empathy" on its way to producing a kind of rhetorical empathy as part of a symbolic deliberative democracy; that the play was premiered by TFA only underscores the critical connection of the liberal-democratic western context to this production.

• • •

Though I lived in the DC area at the time, was working on the chapter from which my first publication on verbatim theater would be excerpted, and had even attended TFA performances before, I wasn't aware of *Children of War* until after the performance. I wasn't there to witness these stories from the mouths of the children who experienced them, the children who embodied the lived experience implied by their narratives. I did not have the opportunity to experience the kind of affective intersubjectivity that both Ritivoi and Dolan identify in these kinds of performances. And while I have since been present for other *Undesirable Elements* performances, for me, *Children of War* can produce feeling and outrage, but since I was not there, perhaps not the kind of deep empathy for the Other that tends to foreground productions of this sort. While that production engaged less ambivalently in rhetorical empathy than did other attempts at empathetic verbatim theater during the Bush years—productions fraught with ambivalence on obviously political subjects, like how to engage ethnic, religious, and ideological difference—empathy found somewhat less anxious territory in representing embodied difference during the Obama era, in productions that made illness, and physical and cognitive disability the thematic center of their deliberations. These performances, like Anna Deavere Smith's *Let Me Down Easy*, Judith Thompson's *R.A.R.E*, and Ping Chong's *Inside/Out . . . Voices from the Disability Community*, underscore a belief in the notion of empathy as rooted directly in embodiment, in a unified body-mind, and in the ways that culture inflects our embodied human responses to the world.[41] And they also reflect more than this, in their deep investment in theater's perceived potential to catalyze empathetic responses, not just in rhetorical storytelling, but in live, embodied enactment.

When I talk about *empathy as rooted directly in embodiment*, I mean this in several ways simultaneously. First, there is the historical origin of the concept in the 19th-century psychological idea of *Einfühlung*: literally, "feeling into" or "in-feeling." Early notions of this form theorized the ways that humans projected physical sensations onto objects, or soon thereafter, how humans sympathetically felt sensations that they observed in others. Initially applied to aesthetics in continental European discussions, the term found its way into early phenomenology, and by the time it was translated into English as "empathy" in the early decades of the 20th century, it was understood (at least in one way) as kinesthetic empathy, and brought into the public eye through the dance criticism of *New York Times* critic John Martin. Lanzoni details Martin's advocacy of US modern dance through its innovations in conveying the sense of movement itself, recognizing "that modern dance required new and demanding forms of aesthetic reception on the part of the spectator," deploying a language of "empathic dynamism."[42]

"Movement was the most elementary physical experience and dance distilled this dynamism into art," Lanzoni notes, showing how Martin "educated his audience to be empathic viewers and not idle spectators."[43]

This sense of the empathetic experience of movement in the performing arts did not remain central to discussions of empathy in the psychological sciences through the popular emergence of the concept of empathy in the second half of the 20th century, but it seems to have remained popularly central to understanding how performance both acts upon audiences and requires empathetic imagination on the part of actors. Only when the conversation on empathy returned to embodiment in the last few decades through cognitive neuroscience and the discovery of mirror neurons did this embodied conception re-emerge: more specifically, "a putative mirror neuron system in the human brain" that "fire in a simulation of another's action, a mechanism that allows us to directly grasp the meaning and sometimes even the intention of a perceived action."[44] Over the past few decades, neuroscience researchers have thrilled at the notion of a neurocognitive component to empathy, though as many studies note, definitions of empathy range wildly, including affective empathy, cognitive empathy (or perspective taking), emotional contagion, guilt, emotional regulation of empathetic responses, and even helping.[45] Recent research also suggests that these embodied experiences of empathy reflect cultural biases that may enhance in-group empathy among people of similar identities, and inhibit it when identities are perceived across difference. In a review article on the subject, Robert Eres and Pascal Molenberghs conclude that "Seeing as group membership modulates responses at each component of empathy, future investigations should identify methods of reversing these biases."[46]

This is a rather dry response to the apparent conclusion that we have pre-existing resistances to empathy across difference, but the gambit of verbatim performances is thoroughly invested in modeling "methods of reversing these biases." Indeed, as a field we have operated on a vague notion that theatrical performance, which frequently combines narrative empathy with kinesthetic empathy, is the empathetic education *par excellence*. We see this in the historical alignment of John Martin's notion that modern dance requires kinesthetic empathy of its spectators with the emergence of Stanislavski and the prominence of method acting in the US, particularly with its deployment of something like empathetic imagination for actorly insight and creation. As Lanzoni brings this history forward from *Einfühlung* to mirror neurons, Rhonda Blair has taken up this connection in her study of cognitive science and acting, which is particularly sensitive to these historical developments.[47] In that work Blair cites then-recent research in neuroscience to think about the embodied bases of empathy as that information is useful for actors, but in ways that, she acknowledges, has potential implications for actors as well. She notes, for example, that "the linkage of empathy and imitation to action, grounded in the physical experience of a moment or situation," is a particularly valuable insight for actors to take away from this research.

While Blair is (rightly, I think) hesitant to draw too-concrete conclusions between this biological basis for empathy and a direct-line path of emotion from character to actor to audience, she does suggest the power of imagining in this way:

> I find it provocative to know that my brain is lighting up in a way similar to another person's and that my muscles are automatically mimicking hers. I find it powerful to believe, based on some evidence, that we could be "wired for empathy" insofar as our bodies and brains mirror each other in terms of perception, and thereby prepare us for action. I find it powerful that imagination, which fundamentally is about the organism having pictures of itself in different situations and contexts in order to know how to negotiate its environment as well as possible, happens not only consciously, but also extensively and richly below the level of consciousness, so that it might be possible to view what we are doing when we're making theatre as helping the viewers' bodies imagine themselves inside the stories we tell.[48]

When she moves on to incorporate the view of evolutionary biologists that empathy may have evolved as a mechanism for collective human survival, she writes compellingly, "Certain mirroring and imitation mechanisms that evolved as strategies in response to survival needs were at their core connective; we had to 'get inside' the other to survive; theatre and performance can maximize high-order ways of doing this."[49]

Though in the past I have been willing to advance this thesis on behalf of verbatim theater in much less careful ways than Blair does, I note that the gambit of such performances hinges on this logic. In reperforming the real stories of others—narratives of suffering advanced as the entrance into a larger societal conversation grounded in the ideals of democratic deliberation—performers are banking on several effects. They imagine the simultaneous deployment of the rhetorical power of empathetic listening, the openness to others engendered through narrative empathy, the ethical imperatives of portraying a different kind of public sphere (a Levinasian one, I venture) based on responsibility to the other, and buttressed by the potential fellow-feeling of embodied empathy that operates at the neurological level through imagined imitation and mirroring. Verbatim performances that focus on disability and chronic illness highlight the convergence of these different lenses on empathy in both the political and the embodied. We can see this both in work such as *Let Me Down Easy*, in which the able-bodied Smith performs different embodiments in ways that might be called virtuosic, as well as in performances such as those produced by Ping Chong and Company, like *Inside/Out . . . voices from the disability community*, in which the performers are speaking their own stories from their own bodies, presenting audiences with the opportunity for empathetic witnessing without the mediation of a listening actor.

Smith's *Let Me Down Easy* is perhaps less highly regarded than her other major works, which have focused on moments of racial violence and the cultural contexts that inflect them, but I would argue that the perceived urgency of those pieces is in part embedded in the historical context in which they were conceived and performed. The national discourse, following what had recently been called "Hillarycare" and would soon become known as "Obamacare," was a logical place for Smith to center her work, as the national discourse on violence and ethnic identity was still focused on international topics (international terrorism and Western incursions in the Middle East that were predicated on confronting that perceived threat), and therefore somewhat escaped the orbit of the artist's "Search for American Character." As I have written elsewhere, though, Smith's famously virtuosic performance of her subjects was tested in the 2009 performance on the subject of exceptional bodies, illness, healthcare, and death.[50] "Exceptional embodiment" exceeded the capacities of Smith's own quotidian embodiment; that is, she was unable or unwilling to perform either the extraordinary physical prowess of athletes and dancers that she interviewed or the particular ways that illness or disability registered in other interviewees' bodies. But what remained in that performance—highlighting the core of Smith's method—is an implicit claim *not* to excellent technical vocal parroting or bodily stylization, but to something like virtuosic empathy. In short, Smith's performance conveys the scene of the interview itself as a palpable location for empathetic sharing of ideas, thoughts, and emotions: rhetorical empathy and narrative empathy twinned in the shaping of a public discourse on healthcare. And where the embodied "in-feeling" resident in historical notions of empathy may feel muted in this production, Smith's method is predicated on that scene of listening that underscores the kind of embodied mutuality that Blair's reading of the neuroscience of acting imagines as a kind of high-order expression of an evolutionary condition for our collective survival.

The relationship between rhetorical empathy and narrative empathy in Smith's practice, then, is very much an expression of the promise that Della Pollock sees in all oral history performance: that the telling of, listening to, and retelling of these personal narratives will be redeemed in some kind of change. By presenting a constructed dialogue that literally embodies and voices diverse identities within a community, Smith narratively and performatively suggests a mode of audience identification through her own use of a storytelling empathy that indeed interacted historically with discussions of healthcare. In this way, empathetic embodiment takes on a new dimension: whereas Smith's tactic elsewhere has embodied diverse racial identities to reveal those categories as arbitrary, the tactic here focuses on the ineluctable fact of embodiment itself, such that this performance posits the human body as a site of, if not precisely universality, then at least human commonality.

Smith's performance begins by presenting bodies that are extraordinary in their excessive performances—Elizabeth Streb, a dancer who accidently sets herself aflame, former heavyweight title-holder Michael Bentt, rodeo performer Brent Williams, the inadvertently hilarious Lance Armstrong—and with monologues that tend to focus on resilience, competitiveness, toughness, and survival as human traits.[51] Resilience transforms over the course of several monologues from bodies testing the limits of human ability to corporeal resilience in the face of illness or injury. By presenting oral history monologues of both exceptionally talented bodies and bodies made exceptional by illness and disability (all under the auspices of her own able-bodied persona), Smith elicits not only a narrative empathy through the stories and enactments of her interview subjects, but invokes what bioethicist Susan Stocker calls "mutuality."[52] Anticipating both Ritivoi's and Blair's claims, Stocker's work claims that mutuality is a recognition of and compassion for a human sameness that creates empathetic attachment and mutual support for those in physical need, an attachment that some evolutionary anthropologists claim is written into a pan-hominid genetic code. The existence of this attachment seems to be confirmed by recent cognitive studies, suggesting that witnessing embodied pain invokes empathetic neurological responses that have evolutionary benefits in the formation of mutually cooperative bonds among humans.

Whether we believe that mutuality is a genetic imperative or perhaps merely an ethical one, Smith's performance is predicated upon a belief in the imperative itself. In this formulation, that belief appears in the sense that these are narratives that deserve our care, and that they are worthy of the care Smith has offered in the form of hearing their stories, telling their stories, and offering her audiences the scene of her own listening. Through the middle of the script in particular, the interview subjects become more likely to be aging bodies or patients currently in treatment. The monologue of Texas Governor Ann Richards focuses not on the suffering of the body, but on the persistence of daily habit; in this case, eating breakfast and "enjoying every morsel," lamenting that she "can't *hug* people," and extolling the virtues of her hospital that will "handpick doctors that they think will work best with patients."[53] In the production described in the script, film critic Joel Siegel is performed laying down and projected on a screen; he tells jokes about not having long to live—bringing his characteristic gentle humor into focus for audiences who know his TV persona—even as he notes that "The *real* Joel Siegel's a little bit sadder. And lonely."[54] In each of these (and other) monologues, Smith includes a moment when the speaker references Anna-the-interviewer, which draws attention to the monologue as a site of exchange, one that Smith's body redeems onstage. These moments follow Blankenship's notion of staging rhetorical empathy by suggesting a chain of copresence and cofeeling, perhaps most palpable in the Lorraine Coleman monologue, a story of feeling comforted by putting her hands under her mother's arms, an empathetic care enacted by touch, a feeling-together.

While this play enacts an embodied empathy for Smith's audiences, it also seeks to stage democratic deliberation about effective healthcare, for in adopting an approach that bridges corporeal otherness, the play also presents arguments about medicalized practices that treat the suffering body as an object of study or of commerce. The caregivers and healthcare practitioners who appear in the play echo those sentiments specifically, narrating stories that de-emphasize diagnosis, critique bureaucratic profit-driven treatment, and valorize copresence and empathetic care. Hazel Merritt describes a nightmare scenario of a kidney dialysis gone wrong in a hospital where no one could find a nurse or doctor to help. Yale hospital patient Ruth Katz narrates a common bureaucratic problem of records gone missing, solved only when the patient revealed that she was associate dean at the medical school.[55] Stanford medical dean Phil Pizzo ruminates on the cost of care and insurance as an intractable issue.[56] Other caregivers tell stories of delivering care despite these dehumanizing obstacles: a physician working during Hurricane Katrina, a palliative care physician, an orphanage director. These narratives emphasize *being with* patients; rather than treating them as medical objects to be brought back into the conformity of "health," these monologues instead frame the doctor/patient relationship as one of empathy, of copresence, and of care. These are values espoused by the play and in turn enacted by the performer, who might in turn be said to be literally embodying and reperforming a kind of empathetic public sphere embedded in an ethic of responsibility to the Other.

And, significantly, this public sphere is enacted in the presence of an audience in such a way as might be imagined to include them in its deliberative scope. If we take Smith's approach as enacting a mutuality with Others whose exceptional embodiment she cannot fully perform, these effects are made all the more powerful by the juxtaposition against her audience. Specifically, on a Sunday in January 2011, my fellow theater-goers provided an important counterbalance and context: a different kind of virtuosity was on display. Likely because of some combination of subject matter and the matinee performance time, the audience was populated with a spectrum of differently abled bodies, from people simply slowed by age to the traumatically disabled. In their negotiation of the narrow aisles, their interaction with technology, their humane interdependence upon and accommodation of one another, audience members embodied difference in significant, if not necessarily radical, ways.

Those embodiments are put literally on stage in Ping Chong and Company's 2008 *Inside/Out*, in development and performance around the same time as Smith's work. Like Smith's *On the Road* series, Ping Chong's *Undesirable Elements* series is, as Associate Director Sara Zatz describes it, "an ongoing series of community-specific interview based theatre works."[57] The series, which began in 1992, focuses on "the real lives of people who are in some way living as 'outsiders' in their communities."[58] Unlike many verbatim performances, though, the performers are speaking their own scripted words, gathered from prior interviews, arranged verbatim by Ping Chong into a lightly theatricalized script, approved by the interviewee/performers, and then rehearsed and re-performed in their communities—a form that adheres more closely to Amanda Stuart Fisher's definition of testimonial theater.[59] So, like *Children of War, Inside/Out* follows a preset formal path: a chronological narrating of key elements of interviewees' lives and experiences, with different actors speaking lines that offer context and background for the personal experiences of that moment's featured speaker, interspersed with common questions that each speaker answers in turn. While this method does not pose the actor's body as an intermediary listener/performer, the image of the performers speaking and listening in community might be understood as a different kind of model of empathetic witnessing. Meanwhile, the common interview questions that ask nearly universal questions ("Where and when were you born?") establish footholds for establishing narrative empathy, even when other aspects of the stories detail the experiences of living in a community in which speakers' difference is marked out. Finally, the embodied presence of the interviewee/performers heightens the possibility for embodied empathy—a possibility that this performance seems to leverage by focusing on bodily difference.

While Smith's deployment of rhetorical and narrative empathy resides in the scene of implied affective storytelling and empathetic listening that collapse together in her representational body, the community of speakers in *Inside/Out* manages that process by establishing the conditions for rhetorical empathy by listening actively to one another, as well as by articulating within their own narratives direct assertions of common humanity. That is, the kinds of staging rhetorical empathy that Blankenship describes is woven directly into Ping Chong's standard framework for *Undesirable Elements*. First, because actors are staged in a semi-circle in this form, they are set in such a way that they are speaking to the audience as well as to one another. As one performer tells their story, others listen actively, shifting their gaze to the speaker and often nodding or tilting their head in response; smiles and looks of concern or shared happiness appear on their faces. This impacts the audience, too: I noticed that when I saw this production, I often unconsciously mirrored the listening faces of performers who weren't speaking in the moment. I was, I believe, literally empathizing with empathetic listening.

The narratives themselves are designed to build upon this effect. Certainly, there is the generic sense that Ritivoi describes, of narratives of difference connecting a sense of shared humanity precisely because of difference. The narratives in the text of *Inside/Out* offer this in a few ways. The monologues narrate a range of experiences of disability: congenital disabilities that affect the speakers' entire lives (Moebius syndrome, cerebral palsy, hearing impairment); disabilities brought on by events or illnesses (a car accident, a brain tumor, late onset blindness); and even caretaking and advocating for people with disabilities. As in *Let Me Down Easy*, some parts of the narrative involve high-performing embodiment—Blair Wing's high school athleticism, Zazel-Chavah O'Garra's professional dance career—and in doing so offer pathways for able-bodied audience members to imagine their own potential future disability. Further, because these narratives offer many different points of entry, different audience members might find a range of points of identification, and not always around disability: Monique Holt identifies the intersection of her identities as a Korean adoptee and a Deaf person; Vivian Cary Jenkins details both a career navigating sexism and work on issues of minoritized representation in the workplace; Zazel O'Garra narrates the persistent racism that shoots through the culture of professional dance; Matthew Joffe and Josh Hecht both identify ways that tropes of idealized US manhood persistently center able-bodiedness.

As if common humanity were not clear enough through these wide-ranging points of entry and complex iterations of intersectionality, the performers' monologues sometimes assert that commonality outright. Matthew Joffe's sections do this most directly. Joffe lives with Moebius Syndrome, "a rare neurological disorder that is present at birth. Those with the condition are unable to smile, frown, suck, grimace, blink, or move their lips."[60] Because Joffe's disability affects his face most visibly, his narratives understandably revolve around the reactions, sometimes of revulsion, that he receives—a test of Levinas's ethics of the face in quite literal terms. His narratives are full of pretty conventional career successes—he works as a disability advocate and personal counselor in higher education—but set against the persistent doubt, underestimation, and discrimination that attends those with visible disabilities. He tells one story of, as an adult, being held out of a swimming pool for not arriving with his mother. "Lady, I have a double major and speak two languages. What is your problem?"[61] is a laugh line, but it also drives the point home: how many audience members have to declare their educational credentials to gain admission to the public pool? Regarding another instance of a neighbor who goes out of his way to avoid him, Joffe wonders, "I wonder what it would take for him to see me as the same human being he is?"[62]

This sense of narrative empathy depends on the same sense of mutuality that animates *Let Me Down Easy*, but further thematizes it, both in staging and in the narrated content, as complex, a push and pull between independence and interdependence. To be clear, many of the stories told are stories of achievement despite and sometimes because of disability and the social structures built up around disability. But interdependence is also crucial. Josh Hecht, a theater director whose primary narrative concerns being raised by a single mother with increasingly debilitating multiple sclerosis, learns from his mother to be a better and more careful listener, "something I draw on whenever I work with actors and the text."[63] Matthew Joffe's narrative also underscores human interdependence; as someone who works with students with disabilities, he is not just someone who lives with a disability, he supports others who do as well. And this appeared on stage as well, for although the staging was quite static—performers in chairs with music stands in front of them—audiences were introduced in the opening lines to Mindy Pearl Pfeffer, as the voice actress for Monique Holt, who signed along. It was initially tempting for me to think of Pfeffer as offering support to Holt, until I realized that she was offering support to me, in making Holt's narrative accessible to the audience. This sense of shared experience, of empathetic helping, deepens in the structure of the performers' speech. While conventional verbatim theater is often organized into monologues, in Ping Chong's framework, each performer's story is distributed across multiple speakers. For example, as Vivian Cary Jenkins tells the story of her sudden blindness caused by retinal deterioration, she speaks lines that tell her first person story, but these are interspersed with other actors speaking lines that add to the narrative. So while Jenkins narrates the story to the audience, other parts of the story—the historical contexts, the voices of figures who appear in the account, sometimes even her own past utterances, sometimes collective declarations offered by all the performers simultaneously—are delivered through a shared story-telling that works to model what mutuality looks like in other contexts.

Throughout, Ping Chong's script is also clear that these are not simply personal monologues, but narratives to be held in conversation with public deliberation. National policies are interspersed into the chronological narrative, from the 1927 Supreme Court case that allowed for the forced sterilization of people with disabilities through the 1972 Rehabilitation Act and the 1990 Americans with Disabilities Act. These national contexts are included alongside more local actions, such as the 1988 protests at Gallaudet University to install a deaf president of the university, or Blair Wing's civil rights action to get an elevator repaired in her building. The production makes clear that interpersonal acts of mutuality are not disconnected from public policy, and that these are collectively effected by a shared sense of common humanity that nonetheless accounts for difference—sometimes radical difference. The performance seeks, in short, to model an empathetic public sphere.

• • •

I do not know if any or all of these effects—rhetorical empathy, narrative empathy, an empathetic public sphere, even neuro-biological empathetic responses—are actually effective, or even if theater can (as Blair says) maximize each of these in high-order ways. Because as we know, empathy (like our biological bodies themselves) is culturally and ethically ambivalent. If feeling-together is really maximized when we share group identifications with one kind of body over another, does verbatim theater open us to other voices, or simply offer opportunities to rank-order the voices we hear most loudly? Does narrative empathy depend upon an openness that allows us to rest content on *feeling-for* an objectified-albeit-pitiable Other, or one that forces us to *feel-with* another human whose differences become the grounds that spur us to action? Or, as some have suggested, do we experience the exertion of feeling-together as enough *like* action that guilt is assuaged and helping is de-activated? I suspect that these questions are functionally unanswerable, or rather, the answer is: it depends upon the context. Perhaps, we can remain open to empathy when the interpersonal conditions—as well as historical, political, and cultural conditions—for openness are ripe, when the vulnerability that is entailed in acknowledging our common humanity feels safe.

I have argued in this chapter that by foregrounding empathetic witnessing alongside and even above rational deliberation, verbatim theater's bourgeois-liberal ideologies find their primary affective mechanism. Within the context of our neoliberal atomization of selfhood, the form works by activating audience members' individual responses to both individual narratives, and also (as Ritivoi suggests) through the generalizable features of individual speakers distributed across the performance. But empathy—both as a concept to be theorized and an affective structure to be experienced—has an historical trajectory. As the concept has evolved, so too has the way that cultural producers have deployed it; a range of social, political, rhetorical, artistic, and economic contingencies have come into play over the last century and a half. We can read empathy's deployment within the context of verbatim theater as contextually contingent. In the 1980s and '90s, the development of the form cohered around the belief that an affective perspective-taking could create the conditions for political harmony. But that has shifted depending on the political zeitgeist, moving in more pointedly political directions during the war-on-terror years of the Bush administration and then toward the ideological debates of health, disability, and embodiment that framed the Obama administration. *Let Me Down Easy* and *Inside/Out* epitomize both the high-water mark for verbatim theater's affective-political aims and its historical contingency; my reading of these two performances hinges on an optimism that is couched in my experience of them within those ripe conditions. Yet, those performances' clearest hopes, and their simultaneous dependence on tenuous historical conditions in order for those hopes to succeed, points to the political fantasies that they rest upon, fantasies that the next chapter will show coming undone.

As an able-bodied straight white male spectator in the politically-comfortable Obama era, I felt safe and hopeful when I saw Smith perform, and again when I was in attendance for *Inside/Out*, both in 2011. I don't know how safe others felt, others whose right to speak was already vulnerable, or, alternatively, for spectators who might have shared many of my identities though not my politics. I sought to remain open to an empathetic experience of the bodies and stories I witnessed in those performances. I have to imagine, though, that spectators who were open and vulnerable to being affected by those moving performances of disability were not the same spectators who jeered and laughed along on November 24, 2015, when then-candidate Donald Trump cruelly mocked disabled *New York Times* reporter Serge Kovaleski during a campaign rally, performing a grotesque travesty of Kovaleski's embodiments. I struggle to believe that a single person could participate in both of those audiences, so much so, that it felt to me at the time that the moment for empathy as a structure for persuasive political affect was ending or over. But even as my stomach lurched at the callous display of anti-empathy on display in 2015, I also recognize my limited willingness to empathize with those Trump ralliers. That nauseous moment was also a political lurch: toward something different, something more cynical and closed off, something deeply suspicious of the idea of a shared humanity.

4 The Opposite of Empathy Is Suspicion

Early on in her ground-breaking *Empathy and the Novel*, Suzanne Keen tells of an experiment that she ran for her students, to gauge their empathetic engagements with three first-person texts: a scam email, a handwritten appeal for tuition assistance from a student, and a novelistic account of a disabled character in need. Significantly, all three personae of the texts were described as African (Keen teaches in rural Virginia), so cultural and likely racial difference was an element of her informal study. Her goal, she states, was to "test my idea that fiction deactivates readers' suspicions and opens the way to easier empathy."[1] She discovers that readers' responses were, to a large degree, more empathetic within the context of the fictional narrative; the purportedly non-fiction texts, even if ultimately sympathetic, failed, as Keen notes, to "deactivate readers' suspicions."[2] "Their skeptical interpretation" Keen notes, "made them suspicious."[3] While Keen goes on to explore how "the world-making powers" of fiction depend both upon a text's actual fictionality as well as the reader's participatory co-creation, her focus on fiction sets aside an important assumption.[4] That is, for as much as Keen is interested in fiction's ability to disarm suspicion, her very project assumes from the outset that suspicion itself undercuts empathy.

Reading Keen's implicit logic about the relationship of suspicion to empathetic reception hit me like a lightning bolt. For all of my deep hope about the power of verbatim performances to encourage a politically and ethically open process of affective and logical perspective-taking, it turns out that a stance that I had been practicing and teaching for years—critical thinking and skeptical reading—might be standing in the way. While certainly the cognitive equation involved to produce the triumph of suspicion over empathy is complex, it seemed to me in that moment of reading Keen just how thoroughly our skeptical impulses prevent us from witnessing with an openness to feeling-together. And when the cultural conditions favor deep suspicion, and even social and political antagonism, the mechanism that I have understood liberal-democratic verbatim theater to be advancing becomes ineffectual, and perhaps even damaging to its own aims.

From here, it follows to a certain degree that a theater of the real, blending its claims to veracity with its obvious artifice, does little to *disarm* suspicion. Indeed, with its insistent claims to reality—both in its form and in the explanatory logic that typically accompanies these performances—verbatim theater seeks to engage in direct confrontation with that suspicion, and push through audiences' skeptical defenses to achieve an empathy that these performances posit as more authentic and presumably more powerful. But when "collective mediation through narration and audition"—what Lauren Berlant articulates as the bare minimum for participating in an intimate public—occurs in the context of an intractable suspicion, that gambit becomes little more than an aesthetic-political fantasy. "Splitting off political optimism from the way things are can sustain many kinds of the cruelest optimism," Berlant reminds us.[5]

• • •

Here is where this project began. I had spent several years of slowly chipping away at a version of a study of verbatim theater that foregrounded its optimistic empathy as a kind of political remedy—essentially, advancing the same argument that in the previous chapter I have suggested these performances themselves are advancing. I opened the project anew in fall of 2019, just as I was also starting in a faculty position at a new university with an eye to re-establishing my scholarly bona fides. I re-read old work: some published, some presented at conferences, some in "parts on the garage floor," as I was wont to describe the project. I assembled those parts together and sat down to write, producing a new introduction to frame the thinking I had produced over the previous several years. But a feeling of dread attended that writing, a kind of futility that the argument was not only not enough (*who hasn't felt that?*) but maybe wasn't even right. After conversations with friends and mentors, I realized that there was no recourse: the project was out-of-date, out-of-step, and stale.[6] And worse: recent performances in verbatim theater were coming up far short of the potential that I had projected onto their form. The world that my draft described was not the world we were living in. Indeed, I came to understand that my subject was a too-perfect example of Berlant's relations of cruel optimism. The project both made a cruelly optimistic argument (*staging empathy will remedy our politically broken landscape*) and was, for me, a kind of experience of the cruel optimism of careerism (*If I can just finish this second book project, I will feel more comfortable*). The whole moment was deeply demoralizing.

"Now: I could write a *great* essay on why this whole book project is suddenly irrelevant," I said. That essay was scarier and harder to write, but within weeks had become the beginning of this book project.

• • •

The timeline of this project coincides with what the social media zeitgeist took to calling, ruefully, "the darkest timeline." That timeline has included not one but two presidential impeachments, a global pandemic with more waves than we can keep track of, a national reckoning on anti-Black (and other forms of) racism, the rise of QAnon, "The Big Lie," and an insurrectionist storming of the nation's Capitol. Conspiracy theories abound: of global pedophilia rings, of chemtrails, of a "plandemic" caused by an engineered coronavirus, of Hunter Biden's board memberships and his laptop, of 5G towers, of stolen elections, of nano-chipped vaccines, and as of this writing, the Russian invasion of Ukraine. Of course we know that conspiracy theories and suspicious political climates are not new. Indeed, part of why they seem so alarming is the connection to historical patterns that locate similar trends in, say, the fascist regimes of mid-century Europe or various Red Scares in the US. And accordingly, amplified suspicion is not the special province of those susceptible to misinformation (to be clear, misinformation attends political discourse in all corners, even if it seems especially rife in one particular corner these days). Because our recent political discourse has been so distinctly marked by misinformation, by a "post-truth" climate for political discourse, and by new opportunities for bad-faith political discourse enabled by social media, even the most cautious and well-intentioned political subjects might find that nursing a healthy suspicion is an important mechanism for surviving the discourse of the rightward lurch of the last several years.

This heightened suspicion stands in contrast to some of the idealized discourses of past moments of our lifetimes (recognizing the dangers of a *whitewashed* nostalgia that shoots through that claim). We might, for example, historicize the boom in verbatim theater in the nineties as engaging a certain investment in tolerance of diversity, both cultural and political. We can similarly see this investment eroding in our current moment, via political polarization generally, as well as the critical unpacking of some terms once key to liberal discourse: "multi-culturalism," "tolerance," and "diversity." Couched within the imperative to pursue empathy as they are, such terms (the reasoning goes) have proven insufficient to rooting out the kinds of racism and other hatreds they were meant to ameliorate. Largely by allowing for the core principles of social inequities to persist undisturbed, resting on tolerance and diversity has allowed "Others" to participate in civic life, while leaving generally unquestioned the centrality of the wealthy straight white men who have held dominant positions of power in the west for centuries.[7] But as Liz Tomlin (whom I will engage in greater depth below) notes, "the political operation of empathy is now most commonly located in the other's resistance to being understood, thus insisting on a two-way dialogic operation that refuses to permit easy colonization of the other."[8] That is to say: a great danger of empathetic representation lies in precisely this concept—"easy colonization of the other," often for the political and economic gain of those already in power.[9] For as much as empathy might mean inhabiting the perspective of the Other, in the context of neoliberalism that habitation might just as easily be harvested for information and reused for individual gain, and even at the expense of those whose narratives are shared.[10] As much as Tomlin valorizes this insistence on two-way dialogue, though, she goes on to identify its correlary creation of "the spectres of the 'other others' who do not . . . subscribe to the cosmopolitan liberalism of the audience."[11] The politics of suspicion cuts both ways, even though the assumptions and ethics of that suspicion may diverge wildly.

● ● ●

Meanwhile, though Keen's primary thesis about readerly suspicion is posed as an obstacle to the experience of empathy, she frequently couches suspicion as a phenomenon endemic to literary criticism. From a critical revulsion to 19th century discourses on sympathy, to a resistance to didactic deployments of empathy, Keen acknowledges the ways that, as scholars, we have been trained away from empathetic listening and empathetic reading.[12] Keen's own wary framing of critical suspicion prefigures Rita Felski's head-on unpacking of what Paul Ricoeur called "the hermeneutics of suspicion" in 2015's *The Limits of Critique*.[13] Felski's work in this book repurposes Ricoeur's evocative phrase to describe practices that "combine in differing ways, an attitude of vigilance, detachment and wariness (*suspicion*) with identifiable conventions of commentary (*hermeneutics*)—allowing us to see that critique is as much a matter of affect and rhetoric as of philosophy or politics."[14] Even as Felski asks readers to decenter suspicious reading in academic discourse in order to make way for other affects, she avoids posing critique against empathy in the ways that Keen does. Instead, she is asking readers, presumably other scholars in the field of literature, to ask ourselves how we might rethink our entrenchment in the stance of critique, which she regards as second-order thinking, implicitly negative, intellectual in character at the expense of the affective and the sacred, and pitched (falsely, Felski implies) from a position beneath authority, which critique often targets.

"Critique," she writes:

> is not especially well attuned to the specifics of its own makeup, presenting itself as an austere, even ascetic intellectual exercise. And yet it turns out to be a motley creature, a mash-up of conflicting parts: not only analytical but affective, not just a critique of narrative but also a type of narrative . . . not just a stance of stern and uncompromising vigilance but an activity equipped with its own pleasures and satisfactions.[15]

Despite her criticism of critique (she takes care not to fall into the habits of poststructuralist critique itself), Felski is not arguing (not overtly at least) for dispensing with the mode altogether but rather for "mak[ing] room for a richer variety of affective as well as intellectual orientations" and (following the lead of philosopher Richard Rorty) for developing "inspiring alternatives and new vocabularies."[16] Or, more practically, "to articulate a positive vision for humanistic thought in the face of growing skepticism about its value."[17]

This approach to suspicion in scholarship has its appeals, for it creates more space for thinking through the affective components of the arts, something that this project attempts to parse while still retaining some classically critique-oriented features: the examination of political constructions, an attention to discourse, a thorough-going interest in historicity, and a wary eye for the operations of a social climate that feels toxic to our flourishing humanity. I also recognize and hope I am foregrounding the motley nature of this analysis, of its analytical and affective dimensions, of my own indulgence in narrative even as I unpack narratives of utopian uplift implicit in these plays. Yet thinking about Felski's convincing identification of suspicion and critique as central to our habits of thought, we must also wonder about our own roles as scholars and teachers in propagating suspicion as a way—even the best way—of being in the world. That is, we might ask: is the very toolkit we have extolled for decades as the virtue of humanistic study—the thing that Felski identifies as the pervasive paradigm—not just a highly developed blocker for empathy?[18] Or even more so, in its more persistent deployment across the bad-faith media platforms of our day, has the hermeneutics of suspicion not only eroded our potential for empathetic listening, but made it too easily exploited, even dangerous?

I ask this because I read Felski's focus on critique (as the operation of the hermeneutics of suspicion in the form of a scholarly affect) as germane to this conversation about our political affects as well. When she asks, at the end of her introduction, "Why—even as we extol multiplicity, difference, hybridity—is the affective range of criticism so limited? Why are we so hyperarticulate about our adversaries and so excruciatingly tongue-tied about our loves?"[19] we might need to squint only a little to see her frustration extend beyond the scope of literary criticism to the context of public discourse more broadly in the months leading up to the rightward lurch of 2015 and 2016. For even as Felski herself avoids historicization, I can't help but read her urging to get out of the suspicion game as itself symptomatic of the overheating of suspicion in other venues: suspicion of immigrants (Terrorists? Migrant laborers?), of political opponents (Snowflakes? Sheeple? Fascists?), of the legitimacy of public discourse (Trolls? Russian bots? Cambridge Analytica? False flags?). A causal connection between rarified theory and criticism and far more widely encompassing political discourses might be tenuous, but in this moment, we can at least correlate the academy's emphasis on critical thinking with critique's stylized stance in the wild: that is, to some degree, a critical stance without the right critical tools will end up looking like a politics of suspicion without the rigor of careful analysis. Or like Twitter.

• • •

While Keen's early formulation in her book articulates something important about the relationship between empathy and suspicion, and Felski helps us see that suspicious stance pervading our discourse in broader ways, the center of Keen's argument ends up revolving around how, within the context of reading, this affective relationship hinges on fictionality. Her closing words to the study reassert that "the perception of fictionality releases novel-readers from the normal state of alert suspicion of others' motives that often acts as a barrier to empathy. This means that the contract of fictionality offers a no-strings-attached opportunity for emotional transactions of great intensity."[20] By extension, those of us examining verbatim theater are left with the notion that if fiction defuses suspicion, then non-fictional narratives—narratives presented *as real*—leave our skeptical walls up. But more: as *emphatically real* narratives, they distinctly activate that suspicion, which both leaves open doubt not just about the *content* of the specific narratives, but about the possibility of a true story at all. Ironically, the claims to the emphatically real are exactly where verbatim theater has staked its apparent credibility. And while this study has not spent much time on the truth claims of verbatim theater and other theater of the real, those claims have always been central to the discourse on the form, and they intersect at this moment with the form's apparent desire to activate deliberative discourse.

Verbatim theater's reliance on the real, the past, fact, and representation is all predicated on what in 2009 Janelle Reinelt called the "promise of documentary," a promise that she applies to documentary broadly, regardless of medium. She makes three important claims:

> 1) The value of the document is predicated on a realist epistemology, but the experience of documentary is dependent on phenomenological engagement.
> 2) The documentary is not in the object but in the relationship between the object, its mediators (artists, historians, authors) and its audiences.
> 3) The experience of documentary is connected to reality but is not transparent, and is in fact constitutive of the reality it seeks.[21]

In the first claim, Reinelt identifies a clash between realist epistemologies (i.e., that a representation can reliably index the real) and phenomenological engagements, a tension that simultaneously depends upon objective reference and subjective reception. This claim leads into the second, in which this clash displaces the central facts of documentary, themselves effectively reduced to fetish-objects in a politicized exchange between the mediators and the audience. This displacement of the facts by the relationship—the communicative exchange—in turn lays bare the lie of the epistemological realism proposed in the first place: that facts can be transparent, unmediated, true. Documentary, then, according to Reinelt, deconstructs itself on its own terms. And yet, she maintains that its:

> promise is to provide access or connection to reality through the facticity of documents, but not without creative mediation, and individual and communal spectatorial desire. The reality is examined and experienced differentially; it is produced in the interactions between the document, the artist, and the spectator. It is never enough. Desire outstrips what is or can be provided. The shards of the document are tattered and thin. The mediation is always suspect. And yet . . . it has its measure of efficacy; it is a way of knowing.[22]

Despite the impossibility of the realist epistemology that Reinelt identifies in her earliest claim, documentary remains for her "a way of knowing," an epistemology of its own. This epistemology inhabits the contradictions of the necessarily-mediated but nonetheless indexical, past but re-present-ed, recorded but live, transcribed but re-embodied nature of a performance that derives its efficacy from both the connection to reality and the mediation that separates the documentary from its referent.

The promise (in Reinelt's words) of this way of knowing, then, rests upon the contradictions of reference and mediation. But even as most academic critical considerations of verbatim performances have concerned themselves with parsing out these epistemologies—how documentary theaters claim to know and tell something real—my project has been focused instead on the affective and political consequences. I take it as more or less established that verbatim theater seeks to approach the real and the authentic through theatrical representation, but also that the real and the authentic vanish at the horizon. The more we approach them, the further they recede. If we understand, then, that staging the real is at once deeply alluring for theater makers looking to stage public dialogue, and yet at the same time functionally impossible, we can begin to see how verbatim theater produces the conditions for a deep epistemological suspicion, even as it frequently seeks to push through that suspicion to some kind of reliable scene for empathetic witnessing.

Jenn Stephenson makes this case explicitly, arguing that the upshot of this epistemological tension is the experience of insecurity, an experience exacerbated by what she calls our "age of post-reality."[23] For Stephenson, whose *Insecurity: Perils and Products of Theatres of the Real* traverses much the same epistemological territory as this project, this experience of insecurity is the necessary by-product of theater of the real. In examinations of plays about real people, real language, real space, and real bodies, she shows how this sense of insecurity is embraced and thematized: that such plays might perhaps begin by entertaining (and even foregrounding) the notion of an authentic reality, but they frequently undercut that notion by asking an important and related question; "'How did this reality (or realities) come to be?'"[24] This turn strikes me as significant, because the question is an inherently critical one, inviting not only insecurity (as Stephenson avers), but also the suspicious stance of critique that Felski identifies. In this alignment of the critical questioning of our representations of reality, and the unavoidable uncertainty and insecurity that results, we find (I think) the conditions of late neoliberalism, complete with reminders of our own precarity and (in one particular set of Stephenson's case studies) our own isolation.

But Stephenson's book, published in 2019, leaves off right at the moment in which this project began. In her coda, Stephenson considers the stakes for the ways that theaters of the real produce insecurity in this age of post-reality, or "post-truth," as the popular discourse has put it. Indeed, Matt Jones frames this notion through the same kinds of performances that Stephenson analyzes, noting first that "Post-truth and its correlatives—post-facts and fake news—quickly came to stand in for a culture that values emotional attachment and loud opinionating over knowledge derived through evidence."[25] But Jones is also careful to hew to a post-structuralist line of argumentation that holds that objective truth was always a fiction, and that performances like Rabih Mroué's 2012 *The Pixelated Revolution* and Guillermo Calderón's *Kiss* establish this directly. Jones and Stephenson are aligned here, though Stephenson also has in mind Baz Kershaw's concern that this thoroughgoing post-structuralist logic, now wildly misunderstood and misapplied in the general public, will unmoor our theatrical politics.[26] Stephenson's coda ruminates presciently on this future, wondering whether the insecurity that her book has so thoroughly located in theater of the real will render our theater ultimately indecisive and its politics undecidable.

She describes her own feeling of panic about this possibility, in fact, but eventually turns to Ulrike Garde and Meg Mumford's notion of "productive insecurity."[27] Productive insecurity, for Stephenson and others, is explicitly a critical stance, the "troubling" and "problematizing" that Felski sees at the center of our habitual scholarly practices. While Garde and Mumford's concept is applied to accepted ways of knowing (the poststructuralist gambit *par excellence*), Stephenson pushes further, to "extend this argument to suggest that the affects of insecurity are not just something to be endured, but to be embraced and fostered."[28] Her study closes by applying this argument to its most urgent stakes: "I don't think I am overstating the case by saying that this critical work is central to the grassroots exercise of democratic citizenship."[29]

I first read Stephenson's book in the fall of 2019, just as I was returning hopefully to the earlier iteration of this book, and recognized clearly her panic about these doubts, and I—tentatively, optimistically—nodded along as she reached this conclusion about the value of a productive instability. But two very difficult and dangerous years later, I am choked up re-reading those lines, and her closing sentence—"Instead of being fearful, insecurity makes me hopeful"—because I now suspect that this hopefulness is just cruel optimism.[30]

• • •

Stephenson's coda, without the benefit of the several years of ugly hindsight that this project is working under, is nonetheless clear-eyed about the political stakes and the early signs of the failure of this fantasy of democratic governance that theaters of the real have often participated in, even if critically. "We might ask," (and she does) "what the connection is between epistemological uncertainty arising from poststructuralism and recent faux-nostalgic desire for security, as manifested by the Trump campaign slogan 'Make America Great Again' and the Brexit Leave campaign slogan 'Take Back Control.'"[31] One might wish that Carol Ann Duffy and Rufus Norris had more fully interrogated that very connection before assembling the text for *My Country; A Work in Progress*, the verbatim theater performance mounted by the National Theatre in February 2017, mere months after the first Brexit referendum and the election of Trump in the US.[32] The appearance of *My Country* at the National Theatre is almost overdetermined, arriving on the heels of a surprising political result following a long public debate about the inclusion or exclusion of the nation from an international body intersecting with discussion of the inclusion or exclusion of international others in the body politic of Britain itself. Not only did the performance enact the liberal fantasy of democratic deliberation that this book has been describing, it inadvertently provoked the *epistemological* insecurity that Stephenson describes while also thematizing *neoliberal* insecurity. And, significantly, it failed—at providing a glimpse of a democratic utopia, at modeling empathetic witnessing, or even at articulating a sense of verbatim legitimacy—seemingly because as the performance seeks to model the space for neutral democratic deliberation, its audiences (or at least the reviewers) instead expressed a hunger for the political, a desire to dispense with discussion and proceed directly to political action.

The emphasis on verbatim performance as a model for democratic deliberation was fully embraced by *My Country*. The 2017 performance and its paratextual materials emphasized its ethos of representative inclusiveness in the form of personages representing six regions of Britain (East Midlands, Northern Ireland, the North-East, the South-West, Caledonia, and Cymru). The play-text foregrounds voices of public opinion in the form of the "real people" interviewed from each region, which are in turn moderated with a sense of even-handedness embodied by the presiding voice of a female Britannia (who also voices political figures situated in metropolitan London, which as a region is not otherwise voiced in the play). Shauna O'Brien explains that "these political voices thread a timeline through the tapestry of regional verbatim voices, beginning with Cameron's formal announcement of the referendum in 2013 to his resignation after the referendum result, and Theresa May's ascendancy to leader of the Conservative Party and Brexit Prime Minister."[33] Throughout, the dialogue presents affective information from the speakers about the (actual and anticipated) experiences of precarity based on whatever outcome might arise, and then as it narrates the post-referendum reaction, issues an open-ended call for good leadership in navigating the post-Brexit future. "The resulting play," in O'Brien's view, "was . . . deployed as a platform for the voices of this British society and implicitly proffered as a contribution to the discourses of the British public sphere."[34]

Not coincidentally, the play drew together all of the resources of bureaucratic western liberal democracy. The play was staged at the well-resourced National Theatre, which dedicated those resources not just to a comparatively rich staging (at least in the context of the typically sparse verbatim theater style), but also to sending researchers out across the UK to collect interviews and to commissioning a prominent poet—Duffy—to arrange the script. Indeed, the fact that Duffy was at the time serving as the poet laureate of the UK underscores the play's investment in national structures, even as her public position in favor of a Remain outcome (the liberal position, to be sure) had been clear from before the play's construction.[35] Further, the positioning of Duffy as a Remain advocate—situated in the metropolitan capital, a center of the circulation of global economic capital, which itself is *not depicted as participating in the debate*—underscores this sense that the wealthy urban center is seeking explanation for the will of its own provincial compatriots. At the same time, the "utopian" space of this performance is presented as an anywhere-UK civic setting populated with the mythic-allegorical personages of Britannia and "her people." This cast of characters itself seems to evoke a kind of country-house historical pageant, the sort of which Woolf imagines in *Between the Acts*, and which fantasizes a coherent literary-historical national identity, even as some critics suggest that the capital/provinces divide in the play suggests the very impossibility of a national theater at all.[36]

But for all of the resources the liberal democratic nation-state and its arts and culture industry wing brought to bear on *My Country*, the reviews were tepid at best. The headline to Susannah Clapp's two-star review calls the play "laudable but limp," while Aleks Sierz sneers at a performance with "all the acrid flavour of virtue signaling."[37] Michael Billington concedes that the show "is never dull but tends to confirm what we already knew: that the referendum has revealed just how fractious and divided we are as a nation."[38] Mark O'Thomas declares that the play "feels ultimately flimsy and lacking in either radical intention or emotional insight."[39] And although Paul T. Davies's review is ultimately positive, he notes that "the production could have been sharper and angrier."[40] Together, these reviews suggest a kind of civic virtue behind the exercise, but one that lacks both the affective-empathetic impact of other performances in the genre, and the political pointedness that the Remain advocates likely to populate the London theater audiences seemed to seek.

This is to say, for all of the performance's attention to apparent neutrality, the production's construction and reception were remarkably out-of-balance. For all that Norris's avowed attention in the production was "to get out and listen" to the British people, the result is a theatrical exercise in which a humbled London populace turns outward to listen to their country cousins, rather than a model in which the National could model multi-lateral listening across difference.[41] We see a hint of this, for example, in Sarah Crompton's *WhatsOnStage* review, when she observes that "The voices are gently treated, allowing the multiplicity of Britishness to fill the stage, encouraging empathy and a willingness to understand."[42] But this formulation implicitly imagines liberal London cultural producers encouraging liberal London audiences to muster up a gentle empathy for those voices recorded in the regions beyond this metropolitan bubble. Indeed, the play frames Britannia (construed as London and presumably the absent south-east) listening to her people, quite literally, in the opening sequence: "Before witnesses we shall listen to those voices we have gathered and see what we can learn. You are the spirits and hearts of your regions and you honour the voices of our people."[43] Her final words bookend this theme as a straining query: "Do I hear you listening? Are you listening?"[44] Yet for all this emphasis on listening, Billington identifies the overarching affect of the play as being one of "simmering resentment":

> "This makes it all the more surprising that Britannia finally refers to 'changing, feisty, funny, generous islands'. Generosity is hardly the quality that emerges from these raging vox pops. By deliberately excluding London and the south-east, the production also does scant justice to the remain cause."[45]

"Simmering resentment" from "raging vox pops" does not sound like the model of an empathetic public sphere that earlier verbatim performances have sought to model, and that the publicity for the play seemed to want to cultivate. The effect instead reflects a climate of deep suspicion that rendered some well-intentioned but condescending efforts at deep listening ultimately ineffective.

This disconnect highlights an uneasy factor in many of the references to empathy in public discourse—that they are often asymmetrical or even unilateral: you must empathize with me, even as I express suspicion of you. In *My Country*, nowhere is this sentiment clearer than in the section, "The Voices: Leadership and Listening" when a speaker from Cymru declares "No one's listening to me. No one cares what I want" even though that speaker does not address the conditions of any other subject among the play's myriad vantage points.[46] While we might identify good reason for political suspicion moving in any number of directions, research around narrative empathy (at least) has revealed the incommensurability of a suspicious stance with calls for empathy. I am thinking here of the anecdote that Matt

Jones relates when defining "post-truth," which ironically addresses Trump adviser Kellyanne Conway's scolding question, "Why is everything taken at face value? . . . You always want to go by what's come out of his mouth rather than look at what's in his heart."[47] Lanzoni spends an entire chapter on how empathy has historically been drawn into civil rights discourse, and Carolyn Pedwell identifies both anti-racist and feminist calls to empathy as countering neoliberal ideology. Yet when those calls for empathy were deployed to help liberals understand the appeal of Trump to white working-class voters, many of whom were understood to harbor racist viewpoints, some argued that racism is a bridge too far, that racist sentiments and actions disqualified such subjects from the benefits of perspective-taking or co-feeling.[48] The rightness or wrongness of these objections aside, many calls for empathy from liberal-leaning artists suggest empathetic listening as a remedy for power imbalances, but simultaneously facilitate modes of reciprocal listening that may well create danger for the disempowered listener.

We might understand, therefore, that the introduction of empathy to theater's idealized public sphere regularly either demands empathy in asymmetrical configurations, or else risks placing vulnerable subjects in the position of having to listen to sentiments that might well wish the listener's eradication. Lindsay Cummings argues for what she calls "dialogic empathy," which "consists of a constant and open-ended engagement, responding and reacting to the other as actors respond to fellow actors and the audience, audience members respond to actors, and stage managers and other crew respond to subtle (and sometimes not-so-subtle) shifts in pace and performance both on stage and in the house."[49] Cummings locates more than one verbatim exemplar of dialogic empathy in her study, and yet these engagements are fleeting and require us to "actively question our position in these narratives, the positions of the one(s) we engage, and how they shape our intellectual responses."[50] And in a moment in which multidirectional affects of suspicion always threaten to make dangerous, even violent, the occasion for intimate deliberation, we can see quite clearly how verbatim performance met its limits in the context into which *My Country* was devised.

The result is, as Stephenson's framework offers us, a through-current of insecurity from start to finish. If generosity and resentment signify empathy's asymmetry in this play, its performance produced, by contrast, symmetrical effects of uncertainty. For set against one another in this particular discourse are the degree to which economic precarity coursed through the entire Brexit debate (marked as it was by national, ideological, and ethnic scapegoating), and the sense that the play's heavily worked verbatim structure created occasions for epistemological doubt that Stephenson sees as crucial for the functioning of a democracy in post-truth times, and which I see (also and alternatively) as symptomatic of the neoliberal moment that tends to reduce subjects to their economic productivity and renders their isolation and the in-it-for-yourself-ness that underscores the simmering resentment of the play. Thematically, this precarity cuts through the play. A section entitled "The Voices: Hardship" addresses rising economic costs directly. Regional voices talking about hard work, losing local industry, and being priced out of food and petrol, are set against a Boris Johnson metaphor about cornflakes in a packet having the opportunity to "rustle and hustle their way to the top."[51] But the economic individual is also foregrounded in discussions of Europe, of immigration, and of leadership. If resentment simmers, that resentment is about scarcity, austerity, and the sense that someone else always has more.

For audiences, that instability may or may not be economic (though audiences at the National Theatre do tend toward economic comfort), but it is produced through the framing of these voices as "real." Indeed, O'Brien notes that the PR around the play focused intently on these voices from the provinces as not only unvarnished reality, but as representatives of "lived experience," a notion that she argues both signals a distrust in language as a source of value or reliability, and also undermines itself by relying specifically on language for representation. Further, she notes, the fact that these voices are framed within the specific thematic issues propagated through the existing media and political discourse, reduces these "real people" and their "lived experience" to something quite different: linguistic soundbites consumable for a mediatized political landscape. The result is an inflated sense of language as a signal of the real, yet one that ultimately betrays its own emptiness. "Perhaps the loss that *My Country* is [mourning]," she muses, "is actually that 'claim to veracity' not of its verbatim voices but of language itself, a loss that I would argue is reflected rather than (as Norris claims) redressed in *My Country*."[52] This is a quintessentially post-structuralist read of the play, but one that connects directly to Stephenson's understanding of recent Theater of the Real in this context. For O'Brien, the performance context is a "climate of paranoia"; following Felski, the method is the hermeneutics of suspicion; and following Stephenson, the outcome is insecurity.[53]

• • •

On Tom Nicholas's YouTube channel on theory, politics and culture, the performance scholar posted a review of *My Country* that encapsulated what other reviews describe as a lack of "radical intention" or pointed anger. The "limp" tenor and "flimsy" outcome that other critics framed in general terms, Nicholas put more directly: "While the piece was supposed to be urgent, bold, and explicitly political, it felt too often like it was walking on eggshells."[54] In short, the play did not do enough to articulate its own (presumably dissatisfied) position on Brexit, and did not do enough to articulate its own rage at what most Remain advocates saw (and see) as a catastrophic outcome. When explicitly identified as failed political theater rather than as a laudable but even-handed stage for civic debate, *My Country* and other such attempts at staging the public sphere only end up advancing what performance philosopher Tony Fisher describes as a "'politics' designed only to induce paralysis in all who come under its influence."[55] Writing from a conversation that is far more interested in radical performance than liberal-national dramatic theater, Fisher instead advocates for performances of antagonism, for those that advance the critical left politics that collaborator Eve Katsouraki describes as "a praxis that emphasizes 'division' and 'interruption' as internal processes of self-realization or self-valorisation."[56]

Perhaps it is true that our current cultural-political climate is—must be—defined by critique, suspicion, paranoia, and antagonism. If so, verbatim theater is left in the lurch, caught up in utopian thinking about the need to deliberate together, in a way that (as Jodi Dean argues) "remains unable to elaborate a convincing alternative because it accepts the premise that we already know what is to be done—critique, discuss, include and revise."[57] Tomlin examines this problem by asking how using verbatim theater might simultaneously balance "the two political logics of egalitarianism and autonomy" alongside the tensions between empathy and agonism.[58] In analyzing another performance from this period, 2016's *Queens of Syria*, co-produced by Developing Artists, Refuge Productions, and Young Vic Theatre, she unpacks the "egalitarian logic" of verbatim performance and theaters of real people.[59] Here, she argues for the potency of empathy in the neoliberal moment, and is hopeful about verbatim theater's power to activate that impulse. In this context, Tomlin eschews the "easy colonization of the other" and cites Cummings's insistence on dialogic empathy as the key to such performances, especially when they stage non-professional performers, as in the case of Ping Chong's pieces discussed in the previous chapter, or the kinds of testimonial performances advocated by Amanda Stuart Fisher.[60]

Tomlin generally remains open to the possibility of dialogic empathy in performance, but also meditates on the production of shame in performances in which suffering subjects, empathetic spectators, and a third group of culpable cultural actors might be defined by the production. While an empathetic spectator might feel some shame and productively encounter the unknowability of the Other, the process simultaneously produces the "other other"—the figure who does not share what Tomlin calls "the cosmopolitan love of difference" and therefore "is disrupting the liberal consensus in the theatre and whose voice and presence is most often absent in the theatre."[61] This creates a dangerous exclusion, precisely because those "other others" "could be safely critiqued, or even vilified, in their absence from the debate."[62] Admittedly, because this "other other" is often absent, efforts to engage such interlocutors sometimes result in liberal hand-wringing, or worse, in creating more volatile and potentially discursively violent theatrical encounters.

Enter Montreal-based company Porte Parole, whose series of performances entitled *The Assembly* seeks to stage the tensions that Tomlin identifies—between egalitarian and autonomous political logics and between empathy and antagonism—in a direct fashion that raises questions about ethics and responsibility within a climate of deep suspicion and deactivated empathy. Facilitators Alex Ivanovici and Brett Watson, together with playwright Annabelle Soutar, devise a script from a specifically arranged encounter, specific to the city in which the production is staged:

> *The Assembly* started in 2017 as a long-term documentary project. In each touring city, the play's creative team sets up and records encounters in which four strangers of wildly different ideological leanings face off and candidly confront the issues that most divide them. A play script is created from the verbatim content of these recorded encounters and, on stage, actors play the four real-life characters in unique debate-like plays, specific to each city.[63]

The resulting scripts vary, but the English language Montreal production certainly stages antagonism in a way that illustrates the difficulty of balancing the tensions that Tomlin identifies.[64]

The series' framework follows the course of an evening in which two facilitators invite four people who occupy different places along the political spectrum to listen to the testimony of a fifth person who is not part of the evening's discussion—a form that stocks the scene entirely with "little man" figures. After being welcomed to the dinner, the guests answer questions about how they identify politically and personally. They are played the testimony of the fifth person, and asked to write a letter to that speaker, one that reflects four statements on which they might come to consensus: what they identify as the speaker's most urgent concern, something they agree with the speaker on, something they are concerned about, and a question that they have for the speaker. The dialogue is occasionally interrupted by the replay of post-Assembly interviews between the facilitators and individual participants as they reflect on the earlier events, creating some Brechtian distancing that allows Ivanovici, Soutar, and Watson to shape the framing of the event. After the staging of the Assembly itself, the audience is given the opportunity to discuss the issue further in a "long table" format, which opens the six seats on stage for the audience to conduct their own Assembly. To be allowed to speak, audience members must be sitting at the table, but are asked to be conscious of the need to share their place at the table in order to allow others to speak. Finally, the audience learns that the letter composed during the dinner that is represented in the performance is given to the speaker at a later date, which is also staged near the end of the production.

Despite publicity materials that suggest "provocatively, the possibility that the time for listening to each other is over," the format reflects a significant investment in the notion of a verbatim theater as a model of deliberative democracy—a staging of public discourse—but it begins by cultivating antagonism in its selection of politically opposed speakers, rather than by activating empathy through thematized narration of suffering or particular hardship.[65] In *The Assembly—Montreal*, the four speakers include Shayne, who identifies as a queer Jewish anarchist millennial; James, a young man who describes himself as conservative; Valerie, a woman in her 70s who says that she is "A conservative / And / I guess I'm maybe alt-right / Though I *hate* that term"; and Hope, a middle-aged accountant born in Jamacia, who tentatively identifies a liberal, but who also recognizes some danger in discussing politics.[66] The precondition of dissensus between participants sets up the group prompt to respond to an interview with the absent fifth person, whose views set some of the terms for the debate. In *The Assembly—Montreal*, that debate is already vigorous by the time this interview is introduced, and actually has the effect of calming some of the discourse. Structurally, then, the goal of reaching consensus on a letter to this fifth subject creates a goal for deliberation, implicitly staking the performance's experiment in deliberation on the notion that the participants are willing to reach that goal. The opportunity for the audience to join the discussion during the long table session, then, suggests a further underlying faith that this staging of consensus after antagonism will activate productive discussion among the spectators, who, presumably by their attendance at a verbatim performance, are more likely already willing to consider the possibility of consensus.

But for all of the ways that *The Assembly* invests in a dramaturgy of democratic deliberation, it ends up playing out the features of our current dysfunctional climate for deliberative democracy: hostile language, recourse to the rights of speech and appropriate attitudes of respect, and throughout, a deep suspicion that the dialogue itself is enacted in bad faith. Tensions in Montreal begin early on, primarily between Shayne and Valerie, who seem to operate on the outer edges of the play's framing of the political spectrum. This verbal sparring heats up quickly as Shayne defines his affinity for anarchism, distinguishing "no rules" from "no rulers," and the advocacy of a kind of radical democracy "in its purest form."[67] This exchange transitions into Shayne's insistence that Valerie's alt-right views are already out-of-bounds—that the alignment of her stances with fascist and white supremacist ideologies are a threat to his life, and that accordingly, "if you value your life, *Stop being a Nazi!*"[68] And soon after, arguing about the election in the US of Donald Trump, he asks "Should I grab you by the pussy right now?!"[69] The play turns down the tension for the audience by choosing that heated moment to cut to a follow-up interview with James and Hope, but then repeats the line moments later. The threat of violent language is palpable, not just in this moment, but across the whole play, for Valerie's (and to a lesser extent James's) anti-immigrant and sometimes overtly white-supremacist stances implicitly target Black Jamaican immigrant, Hope. Meanwhile, while Shayne's arguments consistently adopt a position that marginalized others are under threat, his most menacing language itself (likely intended as illustration more than actual threat, but threatening nonetheless) gives shape to an angry exchange by redirecting Trump's sexually violent language back toward Valerie.

Meanwhile, as Shayne and Valerie menace one another with their speech, James and Hope seek to dampen the volatility through insistence on respectful tone and on respect for others' right to a political stance. After earlier articulating her sense of danger around political discussions (she insinuates that during her upbringing, politics and other affiliations might have had potentially violent consequences), Hope responds to Shayne's rhetoric by advocating tolerance:

> See all *I do*
> Is I live good with people
> I respect, I just . . .
> (Gesturing to VALERIE)
> She likes Donald Trump
> I respect her belief
> I don't like Donald Trump. . . .[70]

The ultra-right Valerie seizes upon this "belief" as a matter of simple preference, as if the implications of that preference were irrelevant. This tension between the position's substance and its style is also articulated by James, who argues that Shayne has "breached that . . . that respectful atmosphere" while James himself worked to articulate a conservative position "in a respectful way."[71]

But this emphasis on respectful dialogue covers over the bad faith of Valerie's actual positions, which the audience later learns are deeply Islamophobic and clearly espouse white supremacy. Black scholars and activists in particular have long noted the ways that recourse to civil discourse occludes bad-faith arguments, and the fact that several participants refer to respect and civility in the face of fascist positions only illustrates the danger of a too-deep commitment to an aesthetics for civil discourse.[72] Shayne is quick to echo this objection, noting that the endorsement of a candidate is not just preference, but more consequentially, the endorsement of "racist, and violently misogynist views."[73] Valerie chooses near the end of the play to make an early exit, claiming the excuse that her husband is picking her up at a precise time, and then leaving behind her own written answers to the letter's prompts. This choice on her part indicates her authoritarian stance; she chooses to opt out of the consensus-seeking exercise and contributes her own responses on paper without working with others to find even the slenderest common ground. Yet Valerie's bad-faith tactics are met with Shayne's own speech, which might be similarly characterized as bad-faith in the context of an idealized public sphere. He refuses to believe many of the ways that she seeks to soften her positions, and after she leaves, he consistently characterizes her as a white supremacist, in contrast to how she characterizes herself.

To be clear, the script itself frames Valerie as out-of-bounds, as a white supremacist whose views and tactics are not legitimate. Three final scenes before the end of the Assembly reinforce this perception. First, we are presented an angry email sent from Valerie in her car to the facilitators declaring that she has never "met as vile or as disgusting a human being as Shayne."[74] Then, in a staged follow-up interview, Alex (Ivanovici) asks Shayne whether it is appropriate to humanize Valerie's behavior to which Shayne responds, "If you do that / You're normalizing hate speech."[75] Shayne's caution to the facilitators here, and his implicit justification for his own violent speech, is that dialogic empathy in this context is not only difficult but dangerous and perhaps irresponsible. And while the juxtaposition of these two scenes might seem like an even-handed or even neutral presentation, the third scene in the sequence is a replay of Valerie's public speech "in Edmonton" to which she had referred earlier in the evening, one in which she decries the influx of Muslims into Canada, invokes English and Roman lines of cultural heritage, and advocates turning freedom of speech into "our *best weapon*."[76] In short, Valerie is cast firmly in this moment as the play's antagonist, and within the context of a likely left-leaning theater audience, is handed the shame that Tomlin notes is typically accorded "other others."

Valerie may be "cast outside the legitimate terms of debate," in Tomlin's terms, but she is not "absent from the theatre." Indeed, the company has brought her to speak and has given her a space, one that might offer her up for judgment but also offers her a further platform.[77] And "the agonistic tensions of democratic politics [become] violent and obscene" within the framework of the "cosmopolitan love of difference."[78] In fact, Valerie explicitly indicates that she is not always absent from the theater as a spectator: she tells Alex that she had seen one of his and his wife's performances before and that it confused and bored her.[79] The spectre raised by Valerie's dismissive admission is not incidental: it amplifies the danger of the public platform afforded her "obscene" positions by disrupting trust in any liberal consensus that might otherwise emerge in the theater itself. For as *Globe and Mail* critic J. Kelly Nestruck points out, "similar racist rhetoric has already radicalized people in Canada—convinced them to kill, in fact."[80] So, at whom do we direct shame for the conditions for violence that comes from (depending on the logic that we follow) either staging or excluding and shaming the "other other"? On the alt-right firebrand who presses beyond the boundaries of the legitimate terms of the debate itself? On the leftist participant who persistently seeks to cast her out? On the theatrical mediators who choose to represent her on stage in the first place? On those same mediators who reinscribe her through their Brechtian framing as the "other other"? These questions highlight the play's ultimately ambivalent framing of Valerie: her dread of the Other, the play's dread of Valerie as the "other other."

Of course, all of this discursive danger (and the bodily danger that inevitably follows) is staged as the risk involved in facilitating actual public deliberation; *The Assembly* stages a suspicious and antagonistic public sphere instead of staging a utopian and empathetic one. But despite risking this discursive violence, the climate of suspicion may not only defuse the possibility for dialogic empathy, it may defuse willingness to deliberate at all. Reviews of the performance that even mention the long table format at the end of the performance have had little to nothing to say about the content of those events, presumably the postdramatic goal of this dramaturgical structure. We might seek the possibility of dialogic empathy in that opportunity for audience members to engage, but at least one instance reveals a deep hesitation even to engage. Although the planned Assembly at University of Maryland was postponed as a result of the COVID-19 pandemic, a workshop performance in March 2019 is narrated and reperformed at the very end of the script for the eventual planned performance run there, one focusing on racism in the university environment. After the actual long table session, and after the final letter is delivered to the absent participant, Alex and Brett return to the stage to tell the audience about that workshop, where "In the long table discussion after one performance /An African American woman rose from the audience and sat at the table in silence for over a minute."[81] When no one joined her, she offered a moving excoriation of the audience, calling out their unwillingness to engage in dialogue at what has even more clearly become a crucial moment in our cultural history. "There's so much to say," she insists in the updated script, "because you see, my dear fellow Americans, your SILENCE says a hell of a lot!"[82]

• • •

I must imagine that every reader understands that the stakes of inclusive deliberation, the "other other," and the potential for these tensions to become "violent and obscene," are neither merely academic nor purely discursive. The reality of these violent stakes hit closest to home for me in fall 2018, when a man motivated by anti-Semitic hatred massacred eleven people at the Tree of Life Synagogue in Pittsburgh. The immediate connection was by proximity: I then lived and worked just over an hour away from that synagogue, and had a department colleague who was closely connected to that community. In response, I worked with some colleagues at the Humanities Center I was directing to put together a panel on encountering anti-Semitism. Our panelists discussed the historical contexts, their experiences with anti-Semitism, strategies for engaging hatred in the classroom. We condemned the murders and the political climate that led to them. The event was not verbatim theater, but it sought to develop similar kinds of dialogic empathy, and reach the same sort of theatrical consensus, a consensus that implicitly applied shame to those who rejected a liberal cosmopolitan ideology, and explicitly applied shame to this man and those like him.

The shooter, a man named Robert Bowers, seems to have long harbored what one profile called "paranoid theories and violent thoughts."[83] He was the classic "other other" of Tomlin's description:

> "Those whose voices are not permitted legitimacy on the democratic stage are those who have nothing to gain from the cosmopolitan vision of increased mobility and opportunity; those whose only property of value is a communitarian identity that is being placed under threat; those whose sense of belonging and locality has become mocked and degraded by those who have privileged mobility and choice; those who are fighting to secure resources for their own communities in a context of a prolonged deprivation. Such subjects are precisely those vulnerable to the call of fascist extremism."[84]

Bowers was long known to be vaguely anti-government, an enthusiastic participant in casual gun culture, and an avid listener of right-wing talk radio. But those theories and thoughts seem to have been sharpened by an intense participation in the suspicious (and suspect) climate of right-wing social media, where his anti-Semitic and anti-immigrant views not only went unchecked, but were stoked. I more recently learned that I have a closer connection to Bowers than simple proximity: he is the nephew of a close friend of a family member of my own, who was raised and lives in the same area as Bowers did. And I wonder: How did two people—Bowers and myself—so seemingly similarly positioned by family and community context, end up in such polarized places?

This act of horrifying violence was certainly borne of a deep suspicion of Jews and immigrants that was fueled by misinformation and racism, precisely the sort of dread of the Other that is reflected in the discourse of *The Assembly*. Reports of anti-Semitic speech online correlate with spikes in anti-Semitic vandalism and violence, and no one is surprised that this spike dates to 2016, when the rightward lurch happened in the US in earnest. Given that, I wonder about the implied causation of Tomlin's statement about "other others" and the potential of violent political discourse. Couldn't the causation be reversed? *When the agonistic tensions of democratic politics are most violent and obscene, then such 'other others' are most at risk of being cast outside the legitimate terms of debate.* Is that casting-out not a just response? Or is the compulsory inclusion of violent actors in the discourse a necessary but distasteful component of staging the public sphere? Can such a conception ever be utopian? Or does even the possibility of inclusion of these violent interlocutors suggest something rotten at the core of the democracy these performances might be preparing us for?

• • •

During this period, Anna Deavere Smith's most prominent theater work came in the form of 2015's *Notes from the Field*, a performance from her broader *Pipeline Project*, which seeks to call attention to the cycle that entangles young people of color in poverty and the criminal justice system—what we have come to know as "the school to prison pipeline." While I did not have the opportunity to see Smith's performance of *Notes from the Field* live, I was able to see her deliver the 2015 National Endowment for the Humanities' Jefferson Lecture at the Kennedy Center, where she almost casually offered several monologues from the broader project while seated, one leg propped up in a knee brace. She mentioned that she rarely performed work with so little preparation at this stage in her career, I recall, but (she noted) the situation was more urgent than ever. Michael Brown had been shot in Ferguson, Missouri just eight months earlier. Freddie Gray would be arrested in Smith's hometown of Baltimore six days after the lecture. Donald Trump's ride down his escalator was still two months away, and the first performance of *Notes from the Field* at Berkeley Rep took place a month after that. The urgency would only heighten.

Formally, *Notes from the Field* looks similar to her most prominent work of the early 1990s; the civil unrest in Ferguson and Baltimore in 2014 and '15 created unsettlingly familiar contexts for that work. In fact, the first movement of the version of the performance filmed for HBO (and released in 2018) would be very familiar to the theatergoer acquainted with Smith's work from this period. There is perhaps a greater reliance on journalistic footage than before, but the cadence of one monologue to the next is well known by now, the minimal costume changes still suggesting character with merely the slightest bit of framing, the embodied physicality of the characters perhaps a bit less precise. At this point, I have heard Smith speak and perform often enough to be able to parse out her own vocal inflections underneath those of the voices she portrays. And there is, I think, a greater sadness to Smith's entire performance in this version.

The second movement is a shift, though, from the heightened setting of a Baltimore in turmoil to the tranquil Klamath River setting in northern California, where Taos Proctor fishes for salmon and reflects on his pathway through school and prison. The performance follows this new trajectory, taking a deeper look not just at the moments of violence that erupt in cities in moments of great friction, but at the systems that create that friction. As is true for many Smith performances, we meet many interlocutors after Proctor, representing both lived experience and deep expertise. Smith performs educators and incarcerated people, and later dips into an historical recording of James Baldwin for a late monologue. She closes the televised performance with a monologue from the late Congressman John Lewis, who tells two stories of moments of reconciliation, one when a young police chief in Montgomery, Alabama comes to welcome Lewis during an event at a Baptist church in the city and gives Lewis his badge as an act of contrition for the police's absence in Birmingham and Selma and Montgomery.[85] And the second is the story of a South Carolina man, a former Klansman who had himself beaten Lewis during the Freedom Ride in 1961 and who many years later approached Lewis in his congressional offices to ask forgiveness. The monologue is entitled "Brother," and it tells a very different tale of the verbatim theater's "other other" entering the halls of US democracy than insurgents storming the US Capitol on January 6, 2021 envisioned.

Notes from the Field does not offer me much new to say about Smith's work, even in this shifted climate. Smith herself maintains in this project a link between empathy and democracy: on the website for the performance, she includes an essay entitled "Toward Empathetic Imagination and Action" in which she declares, "We must do the work required to make our democracy robust."[86] But I note two things about this performance. First, that the arc from the killing of Freddie Gray to the stories of police in schools and the prison pipeline, and onward to voices from the Civil Rights movement like Baldwin, Lewis, and—in the printed version—today's civil rights leaders like the Equal Justice Institute's Bryan Stephenson, makes clear the link: that young and disadvantaged people of color are in bodily peril today, as they have been across this nation's history, in a direct line back through the danger and violence of the Jim Crow era, the rise of the Klan, and the institution of racialized enslavement all the way back to 1619. Congressman Lewis's stories of reconciliation that close Smith's performance can help us imagine reconciliations of our current violence, although one hopes that they aren't deferred another 50 years into the future like Lewis's were.

The second item to note is that unlike in earlier pieces, Smith has largely dispensed with the appearance of even-handedness. Her empathy is asymmetrical, though unlike *My Country*, Smith is not seeking to create understanding for those who have done violence to our hope for radical democracy, but rather for those who have suffered from that violence, those caught up in the pipeline. The urgency that she described in the Jefferson lecture in 2015 shows up on this stage when Smith largely excises the voices of school police officers, of thin-blue-line advocates, of high school principals demanding discipline. Even when earlier performances applied Brechtian frameworks to such speakers to create space for critique, Smith still performed these people respectfully and in their own words. Here those people are only present in other people's stories, or in video footage of police brutality against young people who stumble into white male rage in uniform. This makes the final monologue in the televised version significant. My first viewings of this performance imagined this final moment, followed by a collective singing of "Amazing Grace," as too-easily sentimental, a sop to what often has felt like an overflow of anger and despair about how little has changed since *Fires in the Mirror: Crown Heights*. But a more thoughtful reading ascertains that Smith has not admitted voices of white rage, advocates for white supremacy, or stalwarts of bureaucratic efficiency onto the stage of *Notes from the Field*. Those voices are only admitted in this final monologue after acts of contrition, the granting of forgiveness, and action toward reconciliation. Dialogic empathy is only possible—forgiveness can only come after Congressman Lewis can call the man who once beat him "brother"—after the "other other" acknowledges a common humanity and apologizes for the violence.

• • •

As of this writing in early 2022, I note that the Robert Bowers case is ongoing, that he was charged in the weeks I was drafting these paragraphs in the summer of 2021, and that one Tree of Life congregation, Dor Hadash, has specifically asked that federal prosecutors not seek the death penalty.[87] Bowers has not, to my knowledge, expressed any contrition.

• • •

HBO re-aired *Notes from the Field* on June 6, 2020, as protesters across the US demanded justice for George Floyd, a measure of justice that would come a year later with the conviction of Derek Chauvin for Floyd's murder, and just over a year too late to save Floyd's life. That rebroadcast felt simultaneously absolutely timely—rarely in my lifetime have I felt so strongly the need for the call to empathetic action—and also futile. For how could empathetic action occur in the face of such deep cultural suspicion? Taken together, *My Country; A Work in Progress*, *The Assembly—Montreal*, and *Notes from the Field* all suggest the inaccessibility of that vision in our current moment. If verbatim theater of the '90s and early 2000s sought to offer us a utopian model of deliberative democracy, set in a reframed public sphere driven by dialogic empathetic listening, then these more recent performances have all, in different ways, backed away from that vision. *My Country* fails to pursue the possibility of dialogic empathy under the guise of "real listening," but all it offers is the same kind of discussion that led to what most on the left understand as the disastrous outcome of the Brexit referendum. *The Assembly* abandons the idea of the verbatim stage as a utopian model, choosing instead to embrace a hope that representing dysfunctional deliberation will help its audiences conduct themselves more productively. And *Notes from the Field* still imagines the possibility for dialogic empathy—for listening to one another, and feeling together—but only after the "other others" take Shayne's advice from *The Assembly*: "So if they change their ideology to not be based on killing me / Problem solved."[88] If only it were so easy.

This project has asked about verbatim theater in the lurch—specifically, how verbatim theater's utopian liberal democratic vision has been left in the lurch first by a neoliberal political economy and more recently in the rightward lurch away from liberal democracy by authoritarian political and cultural actors who traffic in suspicion. We have looked closely at these performances' investments in modeling a public sphere by foregrounding democratic deliberation, and at the utopian conception of theatrical space itself on which to stage that deliberation. And we have considered the many ways that concepts of empathy (both the broadly conceived and the narrowly defined) have been deployed in the democratic dramaturgies of verbatim theater. But the fantasies enacted by these performances are always historically and culturally contingent, and throughout, I have suggested ways in which those fantasies are deployed with bourgeois liberal ideals within a neoliberal context, especially in the English-speaking western liberal democracies (UK, USA, and Canada) that this project has considered most closely. If the performances considered in this chapter are any indication, the form (at least in these established national-cultural contexts) seems threadbare, even as we return to its most prominent entries in hopes that viewing again might help us make some sense of this dizzying moment, or might let us retreat to a past when we believed that deliberating together in a democratic public sphere—*more discussion!*—was the answer to our problems.

Coda

NOSTALGIA; OR, THE PASTNESS OF THE PRESENT

Anna Deavere Smith is back in vogue, for better or for worse. Better, because as a national leader on the arts of dialogue around difficult subjects, and on dialogue around difficult subjects in the arts, Smith has been an important voice in tense times. Worse, because the climate for national discourse is no better—arguably much worse—than it was when Smith first made her name on the national stage. In June 2020, soon after HBO rebroadcast Smith's *Notes from the Field*, PBS followed suit by rebroadcasting their *Great Performances* presentation of her *Twilight: Los Angeles, 1992*. Earlier that year, a revival of *Twilight* at Signature Theatre in New York had been postponed, after her *Fires in the Mirror: Crown Heights* had been successfully revived at that same theater in fall 2019 by the actor Michael Benjamin Washington and director Saheem Ali. Smith has always been an in-demand speaker among theater artists, but her increased presence on the (now often virtual) lecture circuit was noticeable in 2020 and 2021, not least because, alongside the stories of those whom she has brought to the stage for decades, she is now starting to tell her own story more publicly and with more politicized force. In an autobiographical piece in *The Atlantic* in March of 2021 in which Smith details her experience as one of a small number of Black students at a small women's college, she argues, "In our current moment of division, we cannot afford to go forward without looking back. We must excavate history to assess how we learned to restore human dignity that had been ripped away by plunder and slavery."[1]

Like this closing reflection in her recent writing, Smith's renewed prominence in this context—trying to go forward while looking back—draws our attention to the ambivalent time signatures that verbatim theater has always set out. Its utopian impulses have typically softened its focus on the places in which violence occurred in order to clear the boards, as it were, for its vision of an idealized public sphere. But even as that ideal often arrives in the form of the promise of more open dialogue in the future, its backward gaze means that our affirmative vision of the future always remains just over the horizon. Just as Marxist critique has followed Fredric Jameson's dictum to "Always historicize!" and just as Walter Benjamin's *Angelus Novus* is always staring backwards in horror at the wreckage of history, pastness has typically commanded the view of verbatim theater's most lauded entries, even if affecting the future has been its aim.[2]

But the history of verbatim theater itself has floated into the view of its own re-historicizing impulses alongside new projects that examine our recent pasts—going forward by looking back on earlier efforts at looking back.[3] Theater companies have resorted to reviving performances like *Twilight* and *The Laramie Project* as part of the canon, with Smith and Kaufman taking their places alongside, say, Sophie Treadwell and Thornton Wilder as theater makers whose work we re-examine with admiration, with fondness, and with nostalgia. I note with interest the return to these 20th century artifacts of social-political theater as objects of liberal nostalgia—of longing not for the lived experiences of a time past, per se (we're still always historicizing!), but for the representational strategies of a time past, when we still believed in the possibility of a certain kind of future, or that a certain kind of future could be accessed through a certain kind of cultural behavior. I include myself as a participant in this political affect (attested by the tenor of both my earlier work on verbatim theater and the tenor of this very book, too), registering in the experience of nostalgia a structure for experiencing disillusionment as a kind of political grief. But nostalgia is not just an endpoint, because it *is* a political affect, which means that it circulates in our cultural logics, it surfaces in our artmaking through its curious temporalities and emerges sometimes powerfully and even cruelly in the form of political actions and outcomes.

b

Nostalgia (like democracy, utopia, empathy, and even suspicion) can mean many things in many contexts. In general, we tend to use the term to describe a longing for a past that is irretrievable, an aching for a place-in-time to which we can no longer return. Svetlana Boym identifies nostalgia as "a romance with one's own fantasy," and an "affective yearning for a community with a collective memory."[4] Building on Boym, Adam Muller writes that nostalgia "involves a backward glance through history, but not toward a place or even a time that is necessarily real. It is therefore not really historical, although it has been called a 'historical emotion.' It fuels parochial and cosmopolitan, as well as radical and conservative, moral and political imaginations and their projects."[5] While Muller notes its wide political reach, Heidi Schlipphacke notes that it is "generally considered to be a regressive or even reactionary tendency," though "it can also be seen as a necessary outgrowth of the lack of historicity that characterizes postmodernity."[6]

In our political moment in the US, the regressive impulses of nostalgia have often been framed derisively by the left as a desire to return to the good ol' days of the post-WWII boom, a time when "we" (read: straight, white, middle-class men) agreed about America's goodness, the benevolence of government, and the evil of Nazis—also: a time before the emergence of second-wave feminism, the civil rights movement, Stonewall, or the counter-culture. This fantasy of cultural consensus cohering around a period of universal and lawful conformity is echoed in a later conservative fantasy for Reagan-era economic and military power, the sort that eventually outlasted the Soviet empire in a global stare-off. But the left has its fantasies too: for the spirit of the 1960s to be sure, but with a similar echo for the liberal pluralist dreams of the 1990s as well. These fantasies are obviously not just about cultural products—poodle skirts and psychedelic prints and action figures and record albums—but also (and even primarily) about political romances gone bad. For the right, this tends to be a romance about orderly hierarchical power; for the left, about equality in the public sphere.

Seyla Benhabib, writing sometime between *Twilight: Los Angeles, 1992* and *The Laramie Project*, observes:

> Indeed, theories of the public sphere, from Walter Lippmann to Hannah Arendt, from John Dewey to Juergen Habermas, appear to be afflicted by a nostalgic trope: once there was a public sphere of action and deliberation,

> participation and collective decision-making, today there no longer is one; or if a public sphere still exists it is so distorted, weakened, and corrupted as to be a pale recollection of what once was.[7]

That nostalgic trope wasn't necessarily present in the verbatim performances of the 1980s and 1990s, but Benhabib's identification of that seam of longing is trenchant. We long for a time (apparently past, but perhaps never existing) when we could come to the table and hash out ideas and perspectives on our way to a common goal, consensus around the way forward enabled by a process of deliberation built on mutual respect and agreed-upon rules. Yet, if our very conceptions of the public sphere are anchored in an inaccessible past, then we might see more clearly the deep undercurrent of sadness that flows beneath even our most romantic contemporary fantasies, a sense of the irretrievable distance of our utopias.

But in that ostensibly postmodern moment in which Benhabib was writing, the notion of nostalgia as a political affect was already understood as connected to late market capitalism, with Fredric Jameson's reading of nostalgic films as a structural expression of the critical bankruptcy of pastiche, an uncritical recycling of historical style. If, as Jameson argues, stylistic pastiche is historical style emptied of its material content and historical context, only to be repackaged for easy sale in the cultural marketplace, then nostalgia was the whole affective structure for that sale, a feeling projected "onto a collective and social level, where the desperate attempt to appropriate a missing past is now refracted through the iron law of fashion change and the emergent ideology of the generation."[8] In this context, a longing for the past is not just yearning for another time, but a willful ignorance of "genuine historicity," the material, political, and historical realities that attended the changing stylistic fashions (no coincidence: Jameson identifies the 1950s as the epicenter for this expression). In this way, nostalgia is a way to sell off some features of the past, whether commodity fetish objects or political ideologies, while occluding the real damages done under the auspices of those objects and ideologies. Other postmodern thinkers like Linda Hutcheon have taken similar stances on nostalgia's apparently consistent political valences, asking whether a given representation of the past was "an example of a conservative—and therefore nostalgic—escape to an idealized, simpler era," or alternatively, a critically ironic revaluation of the past?[9]

Meanwhile, Boym maintains that there is progressive potential in nostalgia, locating an ambivalence that Hutcheon also notes as the opposing-but-intertwined nature of nostalgia and irony: "What irony and nostalgia share, therefore, is a perhaps unexpected twin evocation of both affect and agency—or, emotion and politics."[10] Boym expands on this notion, arguing that "nostalgia is paradoxical in the sense that longing can make us more empathetic toward fellow humans, yet the moment we try to repair longing with belonging, the apprehension of loss with a rediscovery of identity, we often part ways and put an end to mutual understanding," but that nostalgia is always "tempting us to relinquish critical thinking for emotional bonding."[11] Boym's framing of nostalgic empathy as opposed to critical thinking is a tension that threads across the history of verbatim theater. Is the form sentimental or ironically critical? Does it look at the past with an ironic critical distance, or has it always functionally erased certain material realities (disordered historical place replaced by utopian theatrical space, for example) in order to point us toward a revision of the past, this time with empathy instead of suspicion? And now, we enter (even more fully) a stage in the form's development in which the ambivalent time signature of verbatim performance—a revision of the past toward a more democratic future—is folded over onto itself once again—a nostalgic replaying of our past revisions in order to reframe a terrible present that we hoped we wouldn't encounter. Boym sees that progressive potential precisely here, in what she describes as "creative nostalgia" that "reveals the fantasies of the age, and it is in those fantasies and potentialities that the future is born. One is nostalgic not for the past the way it was, but for the past the way it could have been. It is this past perfect that one strives to realize in the future."[12]

We could easily argue that revivals of the most powerful verbatim performances of twenty and thirty years ago are working through nostalgia in just this creative way, and in ways that seek out that final fold in the shifting temporality of the form—a reframing of the present by adopting the fantasies of the past. For example, reviews of the fall 2019 revival of Smith's *Fires in the Mirror: Crown Heights* suggest that this reframing appears not as a direct call for dialogue, but rather as a more Brechtian skepticism that yields a clarity only available through the distancing mechanism of time. "It's one of the consolations of first-rate art that there is somehow always hope in being able to see with newly unobstructed eyes," says Ben Brantley in his *New York Times* review.[13] Brantley himself describes the performance as walking this line between critical distance and empathetic witnessing, with a new emphasis on distance, noting Michael Benjamin Washington's cool remove for most of the twenty-plus monologues. That remove only disappeared (in Brantley's telling) in the final monologue of Gavin Cato, father of the boy whose death sparked the conflict. Here, Brantley describes Washington's performance as harrowing and poetic, language that critics often use to recount only the most realistic and emotionally moving portrayals. The result, for Brantley, is "an account with which all of us should be able to identify, no matter how little we have in common with the speaker."[14] For all that this revival seemed to articulate a new balance between empathetic nearness and skeptical distance, Brantley's review ends on perhaps a predictably nostalgic note, noting the limits of the form, but also the value that we seek to extract from the production at this moment: "Being able to see clearly—and at this point, to acknowledge how the divisions portrayed here remain so much with us—may not provide any kind of solution. But it lays the enduring groundwork for the kind of sane, open-eyed conversation that is too rarely held *these days* and has never felt more necessary."[15]

"These days" tips Brantley's hand, but he wasn't alone in this assessment. That same "now more than ever" feeling of the relevance of Smith's work pervades Vinson Cunningham's write-up (from the middle of the Broadway-bereft pandemic) of Smith's *Twilight*, even though its planned Spring 2020 run had been shuttered and postponed until fall of 2021. Cunningham's choice of subjects reflected both the comparative lack of content available to a theater reviewer writing through the early parts of the pandemic, but also the perceived relevance of Smith's work through a summer of urgent protests, a summer that began with the televised rebroadcasts of her work that this chapter started with. Cunningham's take on Smith's work as an idealized embodiment of liberal pluralism is explicit: "Smith's plays take pluralism as a given, but subtly synthesize it into a unified whole. (Another way to say this is that Smith delivers in art what America has chronically failed at in practice.)"[16] The bulk of his essay describes watching the PBS broadcast with much of the same response I've had every time I've seen Smith's work. He sees in this theatrical power a kind of political force as well: "A better government than we have would reanimate the Federal Theatre Project and commission hundreds of Smith-style projects, inviting communities around the country into a more complete understanding of themselves."[17] Better government embraces, apparently, the lost artistic forms of the past to reach our utopian goals for the future.

Is this Boym's "creative nostalgia" or a misplaced hope in a tactic that has only been delivered in art, but not in practice? In reviewing the cultural discourses of Brexit, critic Robert Eaglestone repurposes Berlant's notion of cruel optimism to examine the uses of World War II in the rhetoric of both the "Leave" and "Remain" campaigns, settling on the notion of "cruel nostalgia" to describe a shift from a focus on the present of future as the object of hope, but on a resuscitation of the past.[18] Boym and Eaglestone, in posing categories for "creative nostalgia" or "cruel nostalgia," offer two possible ways of understanding our current approach to resuscitating enduring verbatim performances. Diana Taylor's potent formulation offers another: that in replaying these long-past deliberations over long-past events, we are animating the archive of theatrical deliberative democracy in the hopes of introducing deliberative democracy back into our contemporary repertoires.[19] Smith remains a powerful voice for this moment, but will the methods of the (neo)liberal pluralist 1990s suffice in the rightward lurch of our recent past? Or does the moment require something other than deliberative democracy, a deeper and more primal gesture of hailing one another's humanity across deep time and ideological distance, of the sort that Rebecca Schneider proposes, of "Being with. Being among. Response-ability. Hands up."[20] Must deliberation make way for something more intimate and more basic?

• • •

The argument of this book is that plays like *Fires in the Mirror, Twilight: Los Angeles, 1992*, or *The Laramie Project* sought to make an intervention in the shape of the public sphere. I am arguing that moments of horrifying violence occurred in these places—say, Laramie—and that violence demanded the writing of a kind of history, a history that identified injustice not just between individuals, but in the shape of that place's political configuration: its democracy out-of-whack. Some people were permitted to speak in Laramie, and others weren't. Some people could be who they wanted to be in Laramie, and others—specifically Matthew Shepard—couldn't. The version of Laramie in *The Laramie Project* is a utopian version, a no-place version, a St. Elsewhere version, a version enabled by the empty space of the theater to enact a different Laramie in which theater allowed people to tell their stories, to discuss their stories and their views openly and safely, and where those stories and those views would be heard both critically (the ghost of Brecht is never fully offstage) and affectively. And through staging this fantasy of Laramie as liberal-democratic public sphere, an empathetic utopia, *The Laramie Project* sought to effect a world in which that kind of deliberative democracy—inclusive, rational, just, respectful—might more likely become a reality in the future. When I first encountered *The Laramie Project*, I believed in this possibility. When I first saw *The Laramie Project*, I had already been working on writing my first article on verbatim theater, and I argued committedly that the play helped create a more coherent community in places where community was fractured. That process of creating dialogue out of fractured monologues on the way to an idealized public sphere has always been a fantasy, but one I (we?) fantasized about as good and valuable and productive.

When Tectonic Theater Project returned to Laramie around the tenth anniversary of Shepard's death, what they found was deeply ambivalent. They found (as I found more recently myself) that the fence that had become an impromptu memorial had been taken down. They found the same bench on the University of Wyoming campus (underwhelmingly tucked away) that I found, and they found a community debating over how to remember the events of a decade earlier. The tone of that play is not nostalgic, because it does not, by and large, present the events of October 1998 and after in fond fashion. The bulk of the play takes up a critical question: how do we remember these events? Was the murder of Matthew Shepard a hate crime, one that enacted the worst impulses of a society that worked to exclude LGBTQ+ people? Or was it just a drug deal gone wrong, a violent event whose victim shared culpability? The play follows the familiar "moment work" structure that Tectonic has made famous, and stages the interviews (both interviewer and interviewee) engaged in dialogue about the events. Interviews with citizens of the town, members of the campus and the LGBTQ+ communities, the newspaper editor, the police, Matthew Shepard's activist mother Judy, and significantly, the two men convicted of murdering Shepard, collectively seek to establish two things. First, the play works to reiterate that the crime was in fact a hate crime against Shepard as a gay man, and not (as some prominent counternarratives have argued) a robbery and a drug crime. Secondly, it works to highlight the original play's effectiveness at changing the conversation.

The first issue is handled in straightforward fashion, even as the primary plot of the play, establishing that the memory of 1998 is contested in Laramie, and that narratives that minimize or dismiss the homophobia of the events are (alternatively) bad-faith rewritings of the past, a right-wing political strategy, or a community's folkloric desire to write its own more comfortable narrative. This narrative of the play works critically, citing police reports, counter-testimony, and ultimately, oblique confirmation of that hatred from the perpetrators themselves. But threaded through this narrative of contested memory (particularly in the second act) is also some storytelling about the changing public sphere in Wyoming, a discursive space that is (to believe the play) more open and less homophobic than before. One narrative follows campus community members (most notably Zackie Salmon, who appeared in the original play) advocating for domestic partner benefits at the University of Wyoming, an ultimately successful endeavor. In a similar and even more dramatically told narrative, University of Wyoming professor and now state legislator Catherine Connolly tells her story of becoming the state's first openly gay member of the Wyoming State legislature. She relates how one of her "first orders of business was seeing a Defense of Marriage bill introduced in the House," though ultimately defeated in the legislature, largely on the strength of Republican allies joining the vote against the bill.[21] A moving floor speech from a Republican legislator is performed, and depicted as having changed the shape of the debate in favor of LGBTQ+ rights.

The tenor of these moments is hardly nostalgic, though they shed insight into the nostalgic trope of the entire play, a desire to return to the genre's theatrical home, and to recuperate (and indeed shore up) what Boym calls the "affective yearning for a community with a collective memory."[22] And while Kaufman and company are seeking to restore their history of Matthew Shepard and Laramie, rather than "obliterate history and turn it into a collective mythology," there is another meta-history being told in that play.[23] This is a history in which a theater company came to a damaged town, collected interviews with its residents, reassembled them into an empathetic, utopian, deliberative public sphere, and restaged it for the world. In doing so, this company effected positive change in Wyoming and in the United States, even the world beyond. Indeed, two late monologues in the performance signal something important about the political-cultural landscape of the decade or so following *Ten Years Later*. First is the monologue of Aaron McKinney, Shepard's killer and a man who claims remorse only for disappointing his father, but not for killing Matthew Shepard. He brags of his tattoos, swastikas and the word "'NAZI' across [his] lower back—in big Old English lettering."[24] Less revolting, but to me perhaps as chilling, is the tattoo on his forearm: "Trust No One."[25] In this casually narrated detail, we see a wider movement: the suspicion both held by and directed at the "other other," and his concomitant hatred, correlating directly with his total absence of empathy. That character is (to be fair) admitted into the dialogue in this play; his words from the original play only ever appeared in the form of police testimony and court transcripts. But the play's consensus is clear: he is worthy only of shame. One might easily argue that this is true, and perhaps so true that McKinney ought not to have been admitted into the dialogue at all, as an interlocutor out-of-bounds with the practice of democracy in the first place.

The final monologue, even after Judy Shepard's moving interview, is from Romaine Patterson, a major character in the original play, though absent from this play until the very end. She tells of her struggle to actually mourn Matt the person, in contrast to Matthew Shepard the cultural icon. The play's final words are hers: "And that was a distinction that I had to make, making my way through this storm over the years, so that I could hold on to who Matt was to me personally, but also to recognize the importance of Matthew Shepard, and that story, and how it was told and will continue to be told throughout the years."[26] This moment *is* nostalgic, because it lands, finally, not on the real person that Patterson still grieves (or the real person that Patterson herself is), but on the mythos of storytelling for social change.

The published text's description of the initial performance of the play underscores this nostalgic undercurrent:

> On October 12, 2009, Tectonic Theater Project premiered *The Laramie Project: Ten Years Later* simultaneously in one hundred and fifty theatres in all fifty states and eight countries. Presented by each theatre with their own casts, the audience was linked with the original cast's performance at Lincoln Center's Allice Tully Hall via live streaming. In this historic theatrical nod to the Federal Theater Project, the play was seen by 50,000 people in one night.[27]

That staging—with its "historic theatrical nod" to a highly influential Living Newspaper form that Cunningham also valorizes in considering Smith's work (even though that form was not itself particularly successful in its time)—reflects poignantly the affective stance of the moment that we now inhabit, one in which we look back with great longing at a time when we believed that the dialogue and deliberation of an idealized and empathetic public sphere on the liberal stages of New York, Los Angeles, Washington, DC, Toronto, Montreal, and London could remedy the violent world in which we live.

If the nostalgia for *The Laramie Project* that floats beneath *Ten Years Later* were not clear enough, I situate that play (devised in 2008 and staged in 2009) along a timeline that in 2018 saw my current academic home, Colorado State University, perform the play on the twentieth anniversary of Shepard's death in a theater almost exactly a mile away from where he ultimately died in Poudre Valley Hospital in 1998. The next year saw Atlanta company Theatrical Outfit perform the play in repertory with Thornton Wilder's *Our Town*. That particular pairing has appeared on syllabi and in workshops ever since *The Laramie Project*'s explosion across regional theaters in its first years.[28] But now, *Laramie* has caught up to *Our Town*'s nostalgic look on the mundane, the quotidian, and the "little man" who first walked the boards in 1938, when the Federal Theatre Project's Living Newspapers were briefly staged in cities across the US.

This nostalgia culminated, I would argue, in the state roll-call at the Democratic National Convention in 2020, when that televised virtual political convention saw the nomination of Joseph R. Biden for the US presidency, an office he now holds. Wyoming's votes were announced by Matthew Shepard's parents, Dennis and Judy Shepard, overlooking the same landscape where their son was brutally beaten. Here I recognize the ambivalence between Jameson's critique of nostalgia for its elision of the historical real, Boym's contention that nostalgia might still have political value for progressive politics, and Eaglestone's reframing of Berlant to present us with nostalgia's potential for cruelty. The Shepards' video spot reveals dense layers of critique, irony, and rhetorical empathy. First, while the shot creates the suggestion of the place where Shepard was beaten, this suggestion points quietly at the absence of a memorial for Shepard at a spot made inaccessible to those who might come to Laramie to participate in that cultural grief—just as I had mere weeks earlier in my visit to the town. Second, Wyoming voted overwhelmingly for Trump in the general election, and scores poorly on the Human Rights Campaign's State Scorecard, with only marriage equality as a LGBTQ+-friendly marker on its otherwise bleak rating, an inescapable irony in this whole reckoning of place and public politics.[29] Yet finally, Dennis Shepard's speech underscores the importance of empathy as a remedy for this violence: "Joe understands more than most our grief over Matt's death, but we see in Joe so much of what made Matt's life special." The shared suffering of having lost a child—one also expressed in Gavin Cato's final monologue of *Fires in the Mirror*—stands in for an actual politics that feels your pain, and transforms it into action in the form of new law.

Of course, we must note that Biden's election itself—as a political outcome—represents a nostalgic turn for US liberals, who in 2020 had many more progressive candidates ready to take on the highest office in the land. Is it too difficult to think that votes for Biden in the spring primaries of 2020 were simultaneously pragmatic moves, principled choices, *and* a yearning for the comfortably incremental politics peddled by successful third-way global leaders like Clinton, Blair, Obama, and Trudeau? In short, I understand revivals of Anna Deavere Smith's plays and of *The Laramie Project*, and even the high-profile mounting of new work by the likes of Jessica Blank and Erik Jensen, to be part and parcel of the same political zeitgeist that brought us a throwback politician tasked with bringing us back from the rightward lurch, and from the rightmost ledge.

• • •

As my last research task for this project, I flew to New York in November 2021 to see the Signature Theatre production of *Twilight: Los Angeles, 1992*.[30] Smith had updated the script for our current moment, and the production was directed capably by Taibi Magar, and performed by an outstanding ensemble cast of five. So I went in with fairly clear expectations: that I would witness a powerful performance of a script I knew well, and simultaneously feel—and be critically aware of—a lingering sense of longing. After all, a live performance of *Twilight* was where my immersion in this field began. I expected, too, to learn only a little, and even less to feel hopeful. Mostly, these already disappointed expectations were met, but (as live theater often does) the performance still surprised me. Yes, the casting illuminated new corners of the many monologues, pointing to a life for this performance text beyond the performances of Smith herself, and mitigated some of the concerns about cross-racial performance (especially of Asian American subjects) that have felt increasingly out of step over the years. And yes, new arrangements of the monologues, new juxtapositions that highlighted the interplay between one and the next, and—in at least one case—monologues from material collected in the previous year (rather than the early 1990s) all helped audiences make new connections in a new context. But the most telling shift came in a scene that some critics have regarded as the least successful, but which told me most about how this play's central spatial metaphor had shifted from theater-as-public-sphere to a more intimate, and perhaps less public setting.

Certainly the most prominent feature of the performance was the ensemble casting, with five actors of various racial and ethnic identities. Characters still crossed identities in their performances, though with a greater attention to the power dynamics at play; Asian American actor Francis Jue, for example, offered up an affecting portrait of Korean shop owner June Park, a character who in Smith's performances (including the filmed PBS version) trod uncomfortably close to stereotype. But Jue also performed the role of African American opera singer Jessye Norman in a way that created critical distance about privilege and empowerment, and which allowed the prominence of Norman's racial identity to recede just enough for audiences to see race and privilege in productive tension. The result was casting that looked more representatively diverse in a way that met some current popular demands about representation, but also casting that signaled a subtle shift away from the liberal pluralism represented in Smith's singular embodiment of all identities and toward a more politically nuanced (if sometimes less theatrically elegant) acknowledgement of difference and the complex power flows of difference. The results of the ensemble casting were, one might say, somewhat more democratic and somewhat less virtuosic than Smith's standard-bearing performances.

Indeed, if the casting was the premier draw, it might be easy to overlook the impact of textual revisions, which Jesse Green's *New York Times* review suggested occurred "mostly in ways that support the casting at the expense of the drama."[31] This was certainly true when audiences heard an expanded monologue from Cornel West—performed by all five actors as a kind of choral number—open the second act with a meditation on the possibility of hope in pessimistic times. However, if we understand the representation of democracy itself to be "the drama," this binary between casting and drama breaks down in certain ways. Among the textual changes that stood out most to me was the greater prominence of younger Black male voices—especially those of Keith Watson, identified as a co-assailant of Reginald Denny, and Paul Parker, chairperson of the Free the L.A. Four Plus Defense Committee, both performed powerfully by Wesley T. Jones—voices whose anger took on more texture and depth than I had previously experienced. I ascribe this change primarily to a presumed effort on Smith's part to take seriously the anger of Black men, more than to my own slow understanding of how that anger historically had been presented to me by white supremacist discourses as violently dangerous. Regardless, recognizing that both factors may have been in play created a productive kind of critical distance for me as an audience member. Similarly, a new set of monologues from journalist Héctor Tobar (identified as having been recorded with the playwright much more recently) explicitly correlated the events of 1992 with those of 2020, including the murder of George Floyd and the protests that followed. Depressingly, his dialectical image that juxtaposed King and Floyd served to show how little had changed since 1992: how police violence still underscores the disposability of Black bodies, how the protests that seemed like they were going to turn the corner have yielded little substantive change, how the verdict of the ensuing trial was still in doubt despite overwhelming evidence. Yes, the verdicts against the assailants of Rodney King and of George Floyd differed, but almost thirty years have passed, and here we are again. This experience produced for me neither optimism nor nostalgia, to be sure, though it certainly felt cruel—more even to others for whom police violence is a threat than to me. In the end, after nearly three decades of *Twilight* in performance, the whole enterprise felt more than a little Sisyphean.

But within this general sense of an almost impossible political context, the affective experience of the changing shape of US democracy and the waning possibility of a theatrical public sphere was revised in a more specific, telling, and curious way in Act II. In "A Dinner Party that Never Happened," an imagined scene around a dinner table, all five actors spoke lines assembled from the same material that had sourced the rest of the play, but the scene was expressly framed as a dialogue rather than as juxtaposed monologues. Presiding over the scene was the figure of restaurateur Alice Waters, performed by Elena Hurst; each of the other actors played roles (sometimes multiple roles within the scene) articulating different approaches and pathways to addressing racial injustice, all in the supposedly convivial space of food and drink. Green's review suggests that the approach reduced potentially more affecting monologues to "bon mots," and I tend to agree that the scene represented an interesting, if failed, experiment.[32] But it was the construction of the experiment itself that revealed the most to me about the thorny dilemma of democratic deliberation in the theatrical public sphere. Specifically, by reconfiguring these monologues as *dialogue*, the new scene functionally removed the figure of Smith as a listener. Characters might have seemed as if they were talking to one another, but there was no evidence of them listening and actively hearing what else might be conveyed at the table, thus resulting in pithy "bon mots" rather than multilateral conversation. Green's review recuperates this sense a bit by turning the responsibility outward to the audience, closing with "we are all, in a way—and whether we want to be or not—cultural workers. 'Twilight' doesn't just ask us to build empathy but also demonstrates how."[33] The demonstration of how is not entirely clear in this scene, though, as it amplifies *dialogue* while minimizing *listening*, making the substance of Cummings's notion of dialogic empathy harder to perceive rather than easier.

And more than this, the fact that the scene is set as a dinner party amplifies the challenge of our current context. Over these many years, it seems to me, *Twilight*'s spatial metaphor for our utopian site for deliberation had shrunk: from the town hall down to the dinner table. The revision seems to signal that the play has turned away from the idea of a public sphere entirely, and toward, perhaps, Berlant's idea of an intimate public. But even this intimate setting does not foster intimacy: characters' speech seems directed toward each other, but they do not speak back as if they have been listening. I was reminded as I watched this scene of another theatricalized dinner party, Porte Parole's *The Assembly— Montreal*, which ended with precisely the kinds of suspicious resentment that, at this moment in history, seems to undermine the empathy that The Signature production of *Twilight: Los Angeles, 1992* may nonetheless want us to build. I left the theater that night in November feeling a kind of melancholy. I had hoped, secretly, that my cynical expectations would be blasted open, and that like in 1997, *Twilight* would rattle my cage. Instead, an old friend and I went across the street to grab a drink and talked about how hard holiday-table conversations with family would be when our understanding of politics, public health, or even how to disagree with one another were essentially incommensurable.

• • •

A native Delawarean, I am fairly sure that the first time I met now-President and then-Senator Joe Biden was sometime in early 1985, on a class trip to Washington, DC. My classmate at the time was David Burris, whose father John Burris had just lost the 1984 Delaware senate race to Biden. I recall fifth-grade David asking our senator some kind of hard-ball question about Star Wars Missile Defense. At the time, I was more interested in the *Star Wars* with lightsabers, and my parents had been strong Burris supporters, but even so, I cannot help but to associate Biden with a more innocent and hopeful period of my life.

Nostalgia is not, apparently, just for the right wing, longing for a simpler time. But in my case, it is a little-c conservative impulse because it pulls me back to a moment (sometime between my first encounter with Biden and my actual vote for his presidency) when I believed fervently that real social change could result from doing the kinds of middle-class things I already loved doing, particularly going to the theater. I may have felt a bit smug the first time I saw *Twilight: Los Angeles, 1992*, because I didn't feel the resonances of that performance until well afterwards. But I felt hopeful about feminist change when I saw *The Vagina Monologues* a year later, and about change for LGBTQ+ people when *The Laramie Project* came to my campus, and about reversing the damage of the war on terror when I attended *Guantanamo: 'Honor Bound to Defend Freedom.'* I felt an empathetic pull while taking in *Let Me Down Easy* and *Inside/Out . . . Voices from the Disability Community*. And every time, I wrote about that hope, even when the performances did not always live up to my aspirations for them. I implicitly believed at these moments that I was not just witnessing, but truly participating in the kind of theatrical public sphere that Christopher Balme describes, and that these plays enacted the kinds of utopian performatives described by Jill Dolan. I agreed heartily with Jenn Stephenson that these iterations of the theater of the real offered insecure yet absolutely crucial engagements with democracy: unevenly deployed, but ultimately durable. But after the last five years, and especially after the last two, I understand this hopefulness very much through the lens of Lauren Berlant, who reminds us that optimism can be cruel, prompting us to hope for something that binds us, and the lens of Jodi Dean, who points out the ways that democratic deliberation is often a passive replacement for radically egalitarian action. And through these lenses, I understand how that cruel optimism can have transformed retrospectively into a cruel nostalgia.

This cruel nostalgia confronts us at this moment, a moment when we look back with fondness and optimism on a theater that thrived thirty years earlier and wish for a time when we shared those hopes of a utopia where we could deliberate together in a democratic public sphere shaped by empathy and not suspicion. This cruel nostalgia confronts us, too, at this moment when we look back with fondness and optimism on a US politician whose greatest influences came during a moment when we collectively voted for liberal-pluralist, global neoliberal, centrist-democratic leaders with slogans like "I believe in a place called Hope," "Change we can believe in," and "Yes, we can." Even at my most clear-eyed, I still maintain hope in the fantasies that we invest in this theater, one that sometimes calls merely to "strive for good leadership" instead of calling for empowering its people.[34] I still want to invest in theater that pushes audiences toward empathy, that helps us rehearse a better democracy. But we must also acknowledge that the moment for verbatim theater may have passed, that we may no longer be able to look to the past for a model that only gently revised its own past in order to model a better future. There exist, or are waiting to be imagined, emancipatory and egalitarian political dramaturgies that resist indulging in this cruel nostalgia for a day when we believed that an empathetic public sphere was possible. Perhaps those look like immersive performance environments that invest audiences with a sense of greater agency. They might come in the form of the agonistic performances that Tony Fisher, Eve Katsouraki and their volume's contributors describe as testing out new politics through staging conflict. Some of them, I hope, are performances that seek rich dialogic empathy like Lindsay Cummings describes. Perhaps some of those might be the testimonial performances that Amanda Stuart Fisher distinguishes from verbatim theater, or other forms of theater of the real that are flourishing beyond the richly appointed metropolitan theater spaces of the Anglophone west. Can we turn empathically (and emphatically) toward those dramaturgies that imagine wildly new futures, radically democratic ones? Will those guide us ahead or simply deepen the suspicions that provoke the obscene violence of the "other other"? I honestly don't know, because I don't know the future. But I'm looking for them, and I'm ready to move on.

Notes

INTRODUCTION

1. Raymond Geuss, "A Republic of Discussion: Habermas at Ninety," *The Point*, June 18, 2019, https://thepointmag.com/politics/a-republic-of-discussion-habermas-at-ninety/.

2. Jürgen Habermas, *The Structural Transformation of the Public Sphere*, trans. Thomas Burger and Frederick Lawrence (Boston: MIT Press, 1989); Jürgen Habermas, *The Theory of Communicative Action: Reason and the Rationalization of Society, volume 1*, trans. by Thomas McCarthy (Boston: Beacon Press, 1989); and Raymond Geuss, *The Idea of a Critical Theory: Habermas and the Frankfurt School* (Cambridge, UK: Cambridge University Press, 1981).

3. Geuss, "A Republic of Discussion," para. 12.

4. Geuss, "A Republic of Discussion," para. 12.

5. Gregory Mason, "Documentary Drama from the Revue to the Tribunal," *Modern Drama* 20, no. 3 (Fall 1977): 275, https://doi.org/10.1353/mdr.1977.0047.

6. Mason's impulses about the rise of technology as a complicating factor in foregrounding the truth of these truth narratives was prescient, a subject well covered, in particular by Carol Martin, *Theatre of the Real* (New York: Palgrave Macmillan, 2013).

7. For more on the history of tribunal plays within the documentary tradition, see Minou Arjomand, *Staged: Show Trials, Political Theater, and the Aesthetics of Judgment* (New York: Columbia University Press, 2018) and Jacqueline O'Connor, *Documentary Trial Plays in Contemporary American Theater* (Carbondale, Ill.: Southern Illinois University Press, 2013).

8. Gary Fisher Dawson, *Documentary Theatre in the United States* (Westport, Conn.: Greenwood Press, 1999), 130.

9. *Twilight: Los Angeles, 1992*, written and perf. by Anna Deavere Smith, Ford's Theatre, Washington, DC, February 9, 1997.

10. Ryan Claycomb, "(Ch)oral History: Docudrama, the Communal Subject, and Progressive Form," *Journal of Dramatic Theory and Criticism* 17:2 (Spring 2003): 95–121.

11. Ryan Claycomb, "Playing at Lives: Life Writing and Contemporary Feminist Drama" (doctoral dissertation, University of Maryland, College Park, 2003).

12. Ryan Claycomb, "Staging the Inscrutable Terrorist: Brittain and Slovo's *Guantanamo: 'Honor Bound to Defend Freedom,'" Politics and Culture* (2007):1, http://aspen.conncoll.edu/politicsandculture/.

13. Ryan Claycomb, "Voices from No-Where: Space, Place and the Utopian Impulse of Oral History Performance" (Plenary presentation at Oral History and Performance Conference for Oral History of the Mid-Atlantic Region at Columbia University, New York, NY, March 13–15, 2008).

14. Della Pollock, "Introduction: Remembering," in *Remembering: Oral History Performance* (New York: Palgrave Macmillan, 2005), 2.

15. Jill Dolan, *Utopia in Performance: Finding Hope at the Theater* (Ann Arbor: University of Michigan Press, 2005), 2.

16. Ryan Claycomb, "Voices of the Other: Documentary and Oral History Performance in Post-9/11 British Theatre," in *Political and Protest Theatre after 9/11: Patriotic Dissent*, ed. Jenny Spencer (New York: Routledge, 2011), 93–107.

17. Ryan Claycomb, "The Document and the Account: The Dramaturgy of Truth Claims in Oral History and Documentary Performances" (Paper presented for "The Post-Truth Historian" Working Group at the American Society for Theatre Research 2013 Conference in Dallas TX, November 7–10, 2013).

18. Ryan Claycomb, "Exceptional Embodiment in Anna Deavere Smith's *Let Me Down Easy*," in *Critical Perspectives on Contemporary Playwriting by Women: The Early Twenty-First Century*, ed. Penny Farfan and Lesley Ferris (Ann Arbor: University of Michigan Press, 2021), 168.

19. Geuss, "A Republic of Discussion," para. 13.

20. Anna Deavere Smith, *Notes from the Field* (New York: Anchor Books, 2019); Carol Ann Duffy and Rufus Norris, *My Country; A Work in Progress* (London: Faber and Faber, 2017); Alex Ivanovici, Annabel Soutar, and Brett Watson, "The Assembly—Montreal" (Production draft, November 2018; Performance by Porte Parole Theatre), accessed February 20, 2020, https://porteparole.org/en/plays/the-assembly/.

21. Attilio Favorini's *Voicings: Ten Plays from the Documentary Theater* (Hopewell, NJ: Ecco Press, 1995), provides an excellent overview of this era, with both primary texts and valuable secondary sources. Alan Filewod, *Collective Encounters: Documentary Theatre in English Canada* (Toronto: University of Toronto Press, 1987), traces this history particularly in Canada, where he identifies 1942's *Mr. Churchill of England* as the first living newspaper production there.

22. Filewod, *Collective Encounters*, 17.

23. Eve Ensler, *The Vagina Monologues* (New York: Villard, 1998).

24. David Edgar, "Doc and dram: Why has this decade seen the rise of a vibrant theatre of reportage?" *Guardian* (London) September 27, 2008, 18, https://www.theguardian.com/stage/2008/sep/27/theatre.davidedgar.

25. Robin Soans, *Talking to Terrorists* (London: Oberon Books, 2006); David Hare,

Stuff Happens (London: Faber and Faber, 2005); Richard Norton-Taylor et al., *The Tricycle: Collected Tribunal Plays: 1994–2012* (London: Oberon Books, 2015); Ping Chong and Alisa Solomon, *Undesirable Elements: Real People, Real Lives, Real Theater* (New York: Theatre Communications Group, 2012); Carol Martin, Guest Editor, Special Issue on Documentary Theatre, *TDR: The Drama Review* 50, no. 3 (2006), https://www.muse.jhu.edu/article/201932.

26. In addition to important definitional arguments by Dawson and Martin, see also Alison Forsyth and Chris Megson, *Get Real: Documentary Theatre Past and Present* (New York: Palgrave Macmillan, 2009); Jenn Stephenson, *Insecurity: Perils and Products of Theatres of the Real* (Toronto: University of Toronto Press, 2019).

27. The focus here on Western anglophone democracies might suggest, erroneously, that the coherence of this particular history extends to documentary dramaturgies globally, where in fact documentary methodologies proliferate in different contexts with widely disparate impacts. See, for example, Molly Flynn, *Witness onstage: Documentary theatre in twenty-first-century Russia* (Manchester, UK: Manchester University Press, 2020).

28. Another understanding of "democratic dramaturgies" arises from the concerted thinking about the *process* of creating verbatim performances. While my focus is primarily on the theatrical product and its effects, this complementary line of thinking asks careful questions about how theater-makers might invest their subjects with optimal empowerment, and about how the process of devising verbatim performances might enact those values that the performances themselves seem to espouse. Amanda Stuart Fisher, for example, makes a distinction between verbatim broadly, and testimonial theater, which she prefers, and which hands the performance back to the subjects for performance: "Testimonial theatre-making processes draw on very different ethico-political structures compared to verbatim theatre practices that use a predetermined ethics to negotiate the complex process of making theatre out of real people's stories and experiences." Amanda Stuart Fisher, *Performing the testimonial: rethinking verbatim strategies* (Manchester, UK: Manchester University Press, 2020). While Stuart Fisher focuses primarily on UK performances, these issues in a Canadian context find a rich treatment from the dramaturg's vantage point in Lisa Aikman, "Dramaturging Research, Shaping Encounters: Working Methods and Dramaturgical Structures in Contemporary Canadian Documentary Theatre" (PhD Dissertation, University of Toronto, 2019).

29. Emily Mann, "Greensboro: A Requiem," in *Testimonies: Four Plays* (New York: Theatre Communications Group, 1997), 247–330; Anna Deavere Smith, *Fires in the Mirror* (New York: Anchor Books, 1993); Anna Deavere Smith, *Twilight: Los Angeles, 1992* (New York: Anchor Books, 1994).

30. See, for example, Kristie S. Fleckenstein, "Once Again with Feeling: Empathy in Deliberative Discourse," *JAC* 27, no. 3/4 (2007): 701–16, www.jstor.org/stable/20866807; and Suzanne Keen, *Empathy and the Novel* (Oxford: Oxford University Press, 2010).

31. See for example, Dee Reynolds and Matthew Reason, *Kinesthetic Empathy in Creative and Cultural Practice* (Bristol, UK: Intellect Books, 2012); and Susan Lanzoni, *Empathy: A History* (New Haven, Conn.: Yale University Press, 2018).

32. Dani Snyder-Young, *Theatre of Good Intentions: Challenges and Hopes for Theatre and Social Change* (New York: Palgrave Macmillan, 2013).

33. Maybe we didn't start the fire, but it sure feels like the end of the world as we know it. I don't feel fine.

34. Rita Felski, *The Limits of Critique* (Chicago: University of Chicago Press, 2015).

35. Helen Shaw, "The Decade in Theater: Six Closing Thoughts" What Were the 2010s? *Vulture*, December 31, 2019, https://www.vulture.com/2019/12/the-2010s-in-theater-spidey-hamilton-gatz-and-much-more.html/.

36. Stephenson concludes in her final sentences that this insecurity "is central to the grassroots exercise of democratic citizenship" (234). I explore the difference between her conclusions and my own in chapter 4.

37. See, for example, Atlanta, Georgia company, Theatrical Outfit at https://www.theatricaloutfit.org/shows/our-town-and-the-laramie-project/.

38. Didier Ruiz, *TRANS (MÉS ENLLÀ)* (performance at Festival D'Avignon, at Gymnase du lycée Mistral, Avignon, France, in July 2018), accessed February 20, 2020, https://www.festival-avignon.com/en/shows/2018/trans-mes-enlla/.

CHAPTER 1

1. Minou Arjomand, "Performing Catastrophe: Erwin Piscator's Documentary Theatre," *Modern Drama* 59, no. 1 (2016): 49, https://www.muse.jhu.edu/article/611632.

2. Arjomand, 50.

3. Clas Zilliacus, "Documentary Drama: Form and Content," *Comparative Drama* 6, no.3 (Fall 1972): 224.

4. In addition to Favorini and Dawson, for more on Living Newspapers, see John W. Casson, "Living Newspaper: Theatre and Therapy," *TDR: The Drama Review* 44, no. 2 (2000): 107–22, https://www.muse.jhu.edu/article/33003.

5. Paul Nadler notes the unusual construction of the "little man" figure in Abram Hill and John Silvera's unproduced "Liberty Deferred," a Living Newspaper script on the subject of African American history: "instead of a single 'little man' as the audience's representative on stage, *Liberty Deferred* has two young couples, one white (Jimmy and Mary Lou) and one Black (Ted and Linda). While touring Manhattan island, they learn and argue about the history and current status of African Americans, while observing almost forty scenes. These cover the early slave trade, the economics of tobacco and cotton production, constitutional and congressional debates on slavery, Denmark Vesey's revolt, abolitionism, Harriet Tubman and the Underground Railroad, the Dred Scott case, the Emancipation Proclamation, Reconstruction, the Ku Klux Klan, Jim Crow, and African Americans in the armed forces in World War I." Paul Nadler, "Liberty Censored: Black Living Newspapers of the

Federal Theatre Project," *African American Review* 29, no. 4 (1995): 618–19, accessed February 13, 2020, https://doi.org/10.2307/3042154.

6. Jacob Gallagher-Ross, *Theaters of the Everyday: Aesthetic Democracy on the American Stage* (Evanston, Ill.: Northwestern University Press, 2018).

7. Gallagher-Ross, *Theaters of the Everyday*, 6.

8. Gallagher-Ross, *Theaters of the Everyday*, 7.

9. Pollock, *Remembering*, 2, and Michel Foucault, *History of Sexuality, vol. 1: An Introduction* (New York: Vintage, 1990).

10. Louis Althusser, "Ideology and Ideological State Apparatuses," in *Lenin and Philosophy and Other Essays* (New York: Monthly Review Press, 1971), 142–47, 166–76.

11. David Harvey, *A Brief History of Neoliberalism* (Oxford: Oxford UP, 2005), 2.

12. Harvey, *A Brief History of Neoliberalism*, 4.

13. Lisa Duggan, *The Twilight of Equality: Neoliberal Cultural Politics and the Attack on Democracy* (Boston, Beacon Press, 2003), 42.

14. Wendy Brown, *Undoing the Demos: Neoliberalism's Stealth Revolution* (New York: Zone Books, 2015), 10.

15. Christopher Balme, *The Theatrical Public Sphere* (Cambridge: Cambridge University Press, 2014), 5; Habermas, *Structural Transformation*, 221, quoted in Balme, 5.

16. See, for example, Paul Yachnin and Bronwen Wilson, eds., *Making Publics in Early Modern Europe: people, things, and forms of knowledge* (New York: Routledge, 2010); and Paul Yachnin and Marlene Eberhart, eds., *Forms of Association: Making Publics in Early Modern Europe*, Massachusetts Studies in Early Modern Culture (Amherst: University of Massachusetts Press, 2015).

17. Balme, *The Theatrical Public Sphere*, 75.

18. Balme, *The Theatrical Public Sphere*, 17.

19. Balme, *The Theatrical Public Sphere*, 16.

20. Balme, *The Theatrical Public Sphere*, 15.

21. Seyla Benhabib, *Difference and Democracy* (Princeton, NJ: Princeton University Press, 1996).

22. Seyla Benhabib, "The Embattled Public Sphere: Hannah Arendt, Juergen Habermas and Beyond," *Theoria: A Journal of Social and Political Theory*, no. 90 (1997): 15, accessed August 9, 2021, http://www.jstor.org/stable/41802076.

23. Benhabib, "The Embattled Public Sphere," 19

24. Amy Gutmann and Dennis F. Thompson, *Why Deliberative Democracy?* (Princeton, NJ: Princeton University Press, 2004): 7, quoted in Jodi Dean, *Democracy and Other Neoliberal Fantasies: Communicative Capitalism and Left Politics* (Durham, NC: Duke University Press, 2009): 91.

25. Simone Chambers, "Rhetoric and the Public Sphere: Has Deliberative Democracy Abandoned Mass Democracy?" *Political Theory* 37, no. 3 (June 2009): 324, (emphasis added).

26. Iris Marion Young, *Inclusion and Democracy* (Oxford: Oxford University Press, 2000).

27. See in particular: David M. Ryfe, "Narrative and Deliberation in Small Group

Forums," *Journal of Applied Communication Research* 34, no. 1 (2006): 72–93, https://doi.org/10.1080/00909880500420226; and Laura W. Black, "Deliberation, Storytelling, and Dialogic Moments," *Communication Theory* 18, no. 1 (2008): 93–116, https://doi.org/10.1111/j.1468-2885.2007.00315.x.

28. Dean, *Democracy*, 76.

29. Dean, *Democracy*, 76.

30. Dean, *Democracy*, 91.

31. Dean, *Democracy*, 94.

32. Dean, *Democracy*, 94.

33. Atiba R. Ellis, "The Meme of Voter Fraud," *Catholic University Law Review* 63 (2014): 879, https://scholarship.law.edu/lawreview/vol63/iss4/2.

34. Claycomb, "(Ch)oral History," 95.

35. Claycomb, "(Ch)oral History," 98.

36. Claycomb, "(Ch)oral History," 99.

37. Claycomb, "(Ch)oral History," 101.

38. Claycomb, "(Ch)oral History," 102.

39. Smith, *Twilight*, xxiv, emphasis original.

40. Claycomb, "(Ch)oral History," 104.

41. Claycomb, "(Ch)oral History," 106.

42. Claycomb, "(Ch)oral History," 107.

43. NB: I drafted this sentence on February 1, 2020. Brexit had formally taken effect, and the first Senate impeachment trial of Donald Trump had definitively turned in Trump's favor. If the whole project is less than optimistic, these sentences were composed under this political black cloud (one that would only get more pessimistic as the next eighteen months went on).

44. Smith, *Twilight*, xxv, quoted in Robin Bernstein, "Rodney King, Shifting Modes of Vision, and Anna Deavere Smith's *Twilight: Los Angeles, 1992*," *Journal of Dramatic Theory and Criticism* 14, no. 2 (Spring 2000): 130.

45. Norman and Heston do not appear in the Anchor Books publication, but were both performed as part of Smith's rotating cast of characters.

46. See, for example, Charles Isherwood, "Woman of 1,000 Faces Considers the Body," review of *Let Me Down Easy*, *New York Times*, October 7, 2009, https://www.nytimes.com/2009/10/08/theater/reviews/08easy.html.

47. Smith, *Twilight*, 130. We might also note that the PBS Great Performances production of Smith's performance of *Twilight* cuts between Smith's performance of Miller and archival news footage of the riots themselves. Relatedly, Janelle Reinelt discusses the relationship of the journalistic overtones of the video performances in *Fires in the Mirror* in "Performing Race: Anna Deavere Smith's Fires in the Mirror," *Modern Drama* 39, no. 4 (1996): 609–17, https://doi.org/10.1353/mdr.1996.0090.

48. See Claycomb, "(Ch)oral Histories," 118 ff 13.

49. Bernstein, "Rodney King," 130 (emphasis added).

50. Vincent Canby, "When Communists clashed with Nazis and the Klan,"

review of *Greensboro: A Requiem*, *New York Times*, February 12, 1996, C11, https://www.nytimes.com/1996/02/12/theater/theater-review-when-communists-clashed-with-nazis-and-the-klan.html.

51. Rachel Blau DuPlessis, *Writing Beyond the Ending: Narrative Strategies of Twentieth-Century Women Writers* (Bloomington, Ind.: Indiana University Press, 1985).

52. Mann, *Greensboro*, 330 (emphasis original).

53. Mann, *Greensboro*, 330.

54. Lauren Berlant, *Cruel Optimism* (Durham, NC: Duke University Press, 2011), 226.

55. Lincoln Dahlberg, "The Habermasian Public Sphere: Taking Difference Seriously?" *Theory and Society* 34 (2005): 111–36.

56. Young, *Inclusion and Democracy*, 168.

57. Susan Lanzoni connects empathy and racial discourse, particularly in the period in the US leading up to this boom. I argue in chapter 3 that it is no surprise, historically speaking, that empathy is structured as a mechanism for deliberation across difference in these performances.

58. Mann, *Greensboro*, 314–15.

59. Smith, *Twilight*, 6.

60. Smith, *Fires*, 138.

CHAPTER 2

1. Dolan, *Utopia*, 6.

2. Dolan, *Utopia*, 113, 137.

3. Rachel Bowditch makes this observation in thinking about the utopian impulses of Burning Man, that in rehearsing for utopia, Burning Man hosts such diverse participants as to necessarily emplot heterotopic geographies. I follow her in deploying Foucault's term to describe the workings of ideological dissensus within this idealized space. *On the Edge of Utopia: Performance and Ritual at Burning Man* (London: Seagull Books, 2010), 79–80.

4. Pollock, *Remembering*, 2.

5. Dolan, *Utopia*, 13.

6. Dolan, *Utopia*, 17.

7. I find the congruence of Pollock's descriptions of oral history performance with Dolan's thoughts on performance broadly to be remarkable, both because they articulate the same hopefulness in the power of theater, but that their hopefulness is connected to historically contingent belief in the theater as a particular kind of public space for mediating discourse.

8. Dolan, *Utopia*, 13 (emphasis added).

9. Dolan, *Utopia*, 8.

10. Michel de Certeau, *The Practice of Everyday Life* (London: University of Califor-

nia Press, 1984), 117. Yi-Fu Tuan, *Space and Place: The Perspective of Experience* (Minneapolis: University of Minnesota Press, 1977), 179.

11. De Certeau, *The Practice of Everyday Life*, 117. Emphasis added.

12. Bert O. States, *Great Reckonings in Little Rooms: On the Phenomenology of Theater* (Berkeley: University of California Press, 1985), 4.

13. Stanton B. Garner Jr., *Bodied Spaces: Phenomenology and Performance in Contemporary Drama* (Ithaca: Cornell University Press, 1994), 3.

14. Garner, *Bodied Spaces*, 3.

15. Garner, *Bodied Spaces*, 4.

16. By contrast, Garner's project is often most interested in the sorts of performances that he describes as persistently phenomenological—that is, those that seem to represent no other place than space that exists in the audience's field of perception in the theater itself.

17. Pollock, *Remembering*, 3.

18. McKinley, Jesse, "Bringing the High Drama of Real Life to the Stage," *New York Times*, Feb 27, 2000, https://www.nytimes.com/2000/02/27/theater/spring-theater-visions-america-bringing-high-drama-real-life-stage.html.

19. Ben Brantley, "Theater Review: A Brutal Act Alters a Town," *New York Times*, May 19, 2000, https://www.nytimes.com/2000/05/19/movies/theater-review-a-brutal-act-alters-a-town.html.

20. By contrast, the HBO film version of *The Laramie Project* was largely shot on location in Wyoming, bringing TV audiences to Laramie, a phenomenon I'd argue is made uniquely available by video, but also which completely changes the audience's relationship to place. Similarly, the televised version of Anna Deavere Smith's *Twilight: Los Angeles, 1992* added in place-specific elements—TV footage, walks and drives through the sites of violence, etc. Janelle Reinelt's critique of the faux journalistic aspect of these video productions seems to rest in large part on this direct representation of place. See: *The Laramie Project*; directed by Moisés Kaufman; written by Moisés Kaufman and the members of the Tectonic Theater Project (HBO Home Video, 2002), DVD. *Twilight*, directed by Marc Levin, performed by Anna Deavere Smith (PBS Pictures, 2000), VHS. Janelle Reinelt, "Performing Race: Anna Deavere Smith's *Fires in the Mirror*," *Modern Drama* 39.4 (1996): 609–17.

21. Claycomb, "(Ch)oral Histories," 104.

22. Take, for example, the character of Monique "Big Mo" Matthews in Smith's *Fires in the Mirror*. While the published text indicates that the monologue was uttered in the space of Smith's office in a teacher-student context (one with specific power dynamics), Smith writes, "I performed Mo in many shows and in the course of performing her, I changed the setting to a performance setting, with microphone. I was inspired by . . . Mo's behavior in my class, which was performance behavior, to change the setting to one that was more theatrical." The note goes on to indicate that the speech is performed "Speaking directly to the audience, pacing the stage" (35). This theatrical, performance behavior frames Big Mo's language, "You have to

be def / . . . / Def is dope, def is live / when you say somethin's dope / it means it is the epitome of the experience / and you have to be def by your very presence / because you have to make people happy. / And we are living in a society where people are not happy with their everyday lives" (38–39).

23. Dolan, *Utopia*, 114.

24. Carol Martin, *Dramaturgy of the Real on the World Stage* (United Kingdom: Palgrave Macmillan UK, 2010), 19.

25. Garner, *Bodied Spaces*, 137.

26. Garner, *Bodied Spaces*, 135.

27. Elise Swain, "It's Still Open: Will the Guantánamo Bay Prison Become a 2020 Issue?" *The Intercept*, March 3, 2019, https://theintercept.com/2019/03/03/Guantánamo-bay-carol-rosenberg-intercepted/.

28. Ryan Claycomb. Review of *Guantanamo: 'Honor Bound to Defend Freedom.'" Theatre Journal* 58, no.4 (2006): 705. https://doi.org/10.1353/tj.2007.0006.

29. David Welna, "Trump has Vowed to Fill Guantánamo with some Bad Dudes—But Who?" *All Things Considered*. National Public Radio, November 14, 2016, https://www.npr.org/sections/parallels/2016/11/14/502007304/trump-has-vowed-to-fill-Guantánamo-with-some-bad-dudes-but-who.

30. Nuria Mathog, "LGBT youth reflect on experiences in community," *The Laramie Boomerang*, October 22, 2015, https://www.laramieboomerang.com/news/local_news/lgbt-youth-reflect-on-experiences-in-community/article_46702524-6eff-11e5-ab6d-7329bf86b8af.html.

31. "Matthew Shepard Murder Site," *Finding Brokeback*, last accessed November 12, 2020, http://www.findingbrokeback.com/Entering_Wyoming/Shepard_Murder.html.

32. "LGBTQ Memorials: Matthew Shepard Memorial, Laramie, WY," *Finding Our Place: LGBTQ Memorials in America*. National Park Service, February 20, 2018, https://www.nps.gov/articles/lgbtq-memorials-matthew-shepard-memorial-laramie-wy.htm.

33. John Moore, "The Enduring Legacy of 'Laramie,' Two Decades Later," *American Theatre* (26 February 2020), https://www.americantheatre.org/2020/02/26/the-enduring-legacy-of-laramie-two-decades-later/.

34. José Esteban Muñoz, *Cruising Utopia: The Then and There of Queer Futurity* (New York: New York University Press, 2009), 1.

35. I note here that Muñoz does reference Matthew Shepard in *Cruising Utopia*, but does not reference *The Laramie Project* at all. Instead, he narrates a protest in New York City after Shepard's death, a more direct action, taken *in public*, that involved the coming-together of queer people in a way that provoked a violent response from the city. Far from inspiring an imagined public *sphere*, Shepard's death for Muñoz provoked instead a direct public *action*.

36. Berlant, *Cruel Optimism*, 223, 227.

37. Berlant, *Cruel Optimism*, 226–27.

38. Berlant, *Cruel Optimism*, 227.
39. Berlant, *Cruel Optimism*, 259.
40. Berlant, *Cruel Optimism*, 262.

CHAPTER 3

1. Suzanne Keen, *Empathy and the Novel*, 4.
2. Bernstein, "Rodney King," 130; Gregory S. Jay, "Other People's Holocausts: Trauma, Empathy, and Justice in Anna Deavere Smith's *Fires in the Mirror*," *Contemporary Literature* 48, no. 1 (2007): 130, https://doi.org/10.1353/cli.2007.0024.
3. National Endowment for the Humanities, "Anna Deavere Smith: Jefferson Lecture, 2015," *NEH.gov*, https://www.neh.gov/about/awards/jefferson-lecture/anna-deavere-smith-biography.
4. Pollock, *Remembering*, 4 (emphasis original).
5. Berlant, *Cruel Optimism*, 226 (emphasis added).
6. Pollock, *Remembering*, 5.
7. Lina Misitzis, Hanna Rosin, and Alix Spiegel, "The End of Empathy," *Invisibilia*, Season 5, episode 6, April 11, 2019. National Public Radio, https://www.npr.org/transcripts/712276022.
8. Misitzis, Rosin, and Spiegel, "The End of Empathy."
9. Misitzis, Rosin, and Spiegel, "The End of Empathy."
10. Their argument included a crucial interview with comparative literature and cognitive science researcher Fritz Breithaupt. See Fritz Breithaupt, *The Dark Sides of Empathy*, trans. Andrew B. B. Hamilton (Ithaca: Cornell University Press, 2019).
11. Misitzis, Rosin, and Spiegel, "The End of Empathy."
12. Carolyn C. Pedwell, *Affective Relations: The Transnational Politics of Empathy* (London: Palgrave Macmillan UK, 2014), 50.
13. Lanzoni, *Empathy*, 248.
14. Lanzoni, *Empathy*, 249–50.
15. Lanzoni, *Empathy*, 250.
16. David Savran, "Ambivalence, Utopia, and a Queer Sort of Materialism: How *Angels in America* Reconstructs the Nation," *Theatre Journal* 47 (1995): 226.
17. Pedwell, *Affective Relations*, 55.
18. See especially Sara Ahmed, *The Cultural Politics of Emotion* (New York: Routledge, 2004).
19. Pedwell identifies several strands of this argument in current discourse, noting particularly Ahmed's identification of emotions themselves as "effects of circulation" (Ahmed, *Cultural Politics of Emotion*, 8, quoted in Pedwell, 49).
20. Lisa Aikman, "Dramaturging Research, Shaping Encounters," 18.
21. Sorouja Moll, "Judith Thompson's *Body and Soul*: Tactics of Theatre in the Corporate Strategy," *Canadian Theatre Review* 148 (2011): 48, https://doi.org/10.1353/ctr.2011.0076 (emphasis original).

22. Black, Debra, "Dove anti-ageism campaign hits stage," *Toronto Star*. 9 May 2008. Web. Quoted in Moll, "Judith Thompson's *Body and Soul*," 45.

23. Pedwell, *Affective Relations*, 49.

24. Lauren Berlant, *The Female Complaint: The Unfinished Business of Sentimentality on American Culture* (Durham, NC: Duke University Press, 2008), 12–13.

25. Dean, *Democracy*, 91.

26. Dean, *Democracy*, 94.

27. Guoping Zhao, "The Public and Its Problem: Dewey, Habermas, and Levinas," *Journal of Educational Controversy* 8, no. 1 (2014): 10.

28. Zhao, "The Public and Its Problem," 10–11.

29. Benhabib, "The Embattled Public Sphere," 19.

30. Lisa Blankenship, *Changing the Subject: A Theory of Rhetorical Empathy* (Louisville, Colo.: University Press of Colorado, 2019), 21.

31. Blankenship, *Changing the Subject*, 10.

32. Blankenship, *Changing the Subject*, 9–10 (emphasis original).

33. Blankenship, *Changing the Subject*, 35.

34. Claycomb, "Voices of the Other," 106.

35. Andreea Deciu Ritivoi, "Reading Stories, Reading (Others') Lives: Empathy, Intersubjectivity, and Narrative Understanding," *Storyworlds: A Journal of Narrative Studies* 8, no. 1 (2016): 51–75, accessed May 24, 2021, https://doi.org/10.5250/storyworlds.8.1.0051. 52.

36. Ritivoi, "Reading Stories, Reading (Others') Lives," 52–53.

37. Ritivoi, "Reading Stories, Reading (Others') Lives," 61.

38. Ping Chong, *Children of War*, 29. While the original performance featured stories of six performers, the published script only features five, one identity withheld out of concerns for the performer's ongoing safety.

39. Chong, *Children of War*, 33–34.

40. Chong, *Children of War*, 50, 60.

41. Ping Chong and Company have been involved in several additional productions with local performers and their stories that revolve around experiences of disability and/or chronic illness: *Invisible Voices: New Perspectives on Disability* at Theatreworks in Colorado Springs in 2009; *PUSH! Real Athletes. Real Stories. Real Theatre* at the Young Centre for the Performing Arts, Toronto, Ontario (2015), as part of Panamania Festival, happening alongside the Toronto 2015 Pan Am and Parapan American Games; *(Un)Conditional* at Profile Theatre in Portland in 2019; *Difficult Lives* at Tokyo Metropolitan Theatre East in Tokyo, Japan in 2019. I discuss *Inside/Out* here both because I saw it in performance at Round House Theatre in Bethesda, Maryland in 2011, and because that text is published in Ping Chong, *Inside/Out . . . voices from the disability community*, in *Undesirable Elements: Real People, Real Lives, Real Theater*, Theatre Communications Group, 2012, 111–61.

42. Lanzoni, *Empathy*, 82–83.

43. Lanzoni, *Empathy*, 83.

44. Lanzoni, *Empathy*, 251–52.

45. Robert Eres and Pascal Molenberghs, "The influence of group membership on the neural correlates involved in empathy," *Frontiers in Human Neuroscience* Volume 7, Article 176 (May 2013): 1–5. https://doi.org/10.3389/fnhum.2013.00176.

46. Eres and Molenberghs, "The influence of group membership," 4.

47. Rhonda Blair, *The Actor, Image, and Action: Acting and Cognitive Neuroscience* (London: Routledge, 2008).

48. Rhonda Blair, "Cognitive Neuroscience and Acting: Imagination, Conceptual Blending, and Empathy," *TDR/The Drama Review* 53, no. 4 (2009, 204), 102, https://doi.org/10.1162/dram.2009.53.4.93.

49. Rhonda Blair, "Cognitive Neuroscience and Acting," 102.

50. This chapter's discussion of mutuality and further in-depth analysis of the performance's presentation of virtuosity can be found in Claycomb, "Exceptional Embodiment."

51. Anna Deavere Smith, *Let Me Down Easy*, (New York: Theatre Communications Group, 2018), 11–13, 31–35, 27–29, 15–18.

52. Susan G. Stocker, "Problems of Embodiment and Problematic Embodiment," *Hypatia* 16, no. 3 (Summer 2001): 30–55.

53. Smith, *Let Me Down Easy*, 65–67.

54. Smith, *Let Me Down Easy*, 72.

55. Smith, *Let Me Down Easy*, 45–47.

56. Smith, *Let Me Down Easy*, 55–57.

57. Sara Zatz, "Methodology: An Overview" in Ping Chong, *Undesirable Elements: Real People, Real Lives, Real Theater* (New York: Theatre Communications Group, 2012), 207.

58. Zatz, "Methodology: An Overview," 207.

59. Amanda Stuart Fisher, *Performing the Testimonial*, 17–20.

60. Ping Chong, *Inside/Out*, 120. I quote from the play here because these words were vetted by the performers themselves, and so I am choosing to privilege a version that Joffe himself has authorized.

61. Ping Chong, *Inside/Out*, 125.

62. Ping Chong, *Inside/Out*, 153.

63. Ping Chong, *Inside/Out*, 154.

CHAPTER 4

1. Keen, *Empathy and the Novel*, 29.

2. Keen, *Empathy and the Novel*, 29.

3. Keen, *Empathy and the Novel*, 32.

4. Keen, *Empathy and the Novel*, 34.

5. Berlant, *Cruel Optimism*, 228.

6. Although I name her in the acknowledgments, I owe an especial gratitude to

Jenny Kokai for her clear-eyed reading and her patient engagement of this process as I rethought at that moment, well, the whole rest of my scholarly life.

7. I note that when I say "generally unquestioned" I mean by a broader liberal middle-class populace, largely built on white identity formations. By contrast, scholars and activists of color have been pointing out this structural configuration for decades, in part under the contested banner of Critical Race Theory. For one palpable example of how some beloved liberal notions of diversity have come under scrutiny, see D-L Stewart, "Language of Appeasement," *Inside Higher Ed* (March 30, 2017), https://www.insidehighered.com/views/2017/03/30/colleges-need-language-shift-not-one-you-think-essay.

8. Liz Tomlin, *Political Dramaturgies and Theatre Spectatorship: Provocations for Change* (London: Methuen Drama, 2019).

9. The classic example here is the notion of racial capitalism, which describes the way that racial identities are exploited to create market value. See Nancy Leong, "Racial Capitalism," *Harvard Law Review* 126, no. 8 (2013): 2153–226.

10. For Amanda Stuart Fisher, the distinctions between verbatim performance and testimonial performance become important, as the latter "offers theatre makers an important range of strategies that can lay the groundwork for critical forms of ethico-political resistance and solidarity with others," *Performing the Testimonial*, 185.

11. Tomlin, *Political Dramaturgies*, 130.

12. Keen, *Empathy and the Novel*, 48, 131.

13. Rita Felski, *The Limits of Critique* (Chicago: University of Chicago Press, 2015).

14. Felski, *The Limits of Critique*, 3.

15. Felski, *The Limits of Critique*, 118.

16. Felski, *The Limits of Critique*, 150.

17. Felski, *The Limits of Critique*, 186.

18. In my primary field, English studies, we might see evidence of a fatigue for suspicious hermeneutics in the flight of undergraduates from literary criticism one step over to creative writing; (in theater studies, the art-making has been more consistently central).

19. Felski, *The Limits of Critique*, 13.

20. Keen, *Empathy and the Novel*, 168.

21. Janelle Reinelt, "The Promise of Documentary," in *Get Real: Documentary Theatre Past and Present*, ed. Alison Forsyth and Chris Megson (Basingstoke: Palgrave, 2009), 7.

22. Reinelt, "The Promise of Documentary," 22–23.

23. Stephenson, *Insecurity*, 4.

24. Stephenson, *Insecurity*, 17.

25. Matt Jones, "Performing Post-Truth: An Interview with Director Ashlie Corcoran," *Theatre Journal* 72, no. 1 (2020): E-1–E-6, https://doi.org/10.1353/tj.2020.0000.

26. Baz Kershaw, *The Radical in Performance: Between Brecht and Baudrillard* (London: Routledge, 1999), quoted in Stephenson, 228.

27. Ulrike Garde and Meg Mumford, "Postdramatic Reality Theatre and Productive Insecurity: Destabilising Encounters with the Unfamiliar in Theatre from Sydney and Berlin," in *Postdramatic Theatre and the Political*, ed. Karen Jürs-Munby, Jerome Carroll, and Steve Giles (London: Bloomsbury, 2013), 147–64.

28. Stephenson, *Insecurity*, 231.

29. Stephenson, *Insecurity*, 234.

30. Stephenson, *Insecurity*, 234.

31. Stephenson, *Insecurity*, 230–31.

32. Carol Ann Duffy and Rufus Norris, *My Country; A Work in Progress* (London: Faber & Faber, 2019).

33. Shauna O'Brien, "'Divided by a Common Language': The Use of Verbatim in Carol Ann Duffy and Rufus Norris' *My Country; A Work in Progress*," *Humanities* 8, no. 1 (2019): 58, https://doi.org/10.3390/h80100582.

34. O'Brien, "Divided by a Common Language," 2.

35. O'Brien, "Divided by a Common Language," 3.

36. Tom Nicholas, "*My Country* by Carol Ann Duffy and Rufus Norris at National Theatre London | Performance Analysis." *Tom Nicholas: Theory, Politics, Culture*, March 14, 2017. Recording currently listed as private and shared privately by the author. Last accessed July 28, 2021, https://www.youtube.com/channel/UCxt2r57cLastdmrReiQJkEg.

37. Susannah Clapp, "*My Country: A Work in Progress* review—A laudable but limp look at Brexit Britain," *Guardian*, March 19, 2017, https://www.theguardian.com/stage/2017/mar/19/my-country-work-in-progress-dorfman-observer-review. Aleks Sierz, review of *My Country; A Work in Progress*, National Theatre, *Aleks Sierz*, March 10, 2017, https://www.sierz.co.uk/reviews/my-country-a-work-in-progress-national-theatre/. Originally published in *The Arts Desk*, https://www.theartsdesk.com/.

38. Michael Billington, "*My Country: A Work in Progress* review—Carol Ann Duffy tackles Brexit," *Guardian*, March 12, 2017, https://www.theguardian.com/stage/2017/mar/12/my-country-a-work-in-progress-review-carol-ann-duffy-visits-brexit.

39. Mark O'Thomas, "*My Country*: A Play about Brexit that Tries to Break the Bubble but Disappoints," *The Conversation*, March 21, 2017, https://theconversation.com/my-country-a-play-about-brexit-that-tries-to-break-the-bubble-but-disappoints-74388.

40. Paul T. Davies, "REVIEW: *My Country;A Work in Progress*," *BritishTheatre.com*, March 11, 2017, https://britishtheatre.com/review-my-country-a-work-in-progress-national-theatre/.

41. Daisy McCorgray, "My Country: This Brexit play actually listened to people in the UK," *The New European* (3 March 2017), https://www.theneweuropean.co.uk/brexit-news/my-country-this-brexit-play-actually-listened-to-people-in-16920.

42. Sarah Crompton, "Review: *My Country: A Work in Progress*," WhatsOnStage, March 10, 2017, https://www.whatsonstage.com/london-theatre/reviews/my-country-a-work-in-progress-dorfman-national_43092.html.

43. Duffy and Norris, *My Country*, 6.

44. Duffy and Norris, *My Country*, 58.

45. Billington, "*My Country.*"

46. Duffy and Norris, *My Country*, 31.

47. Quoted in Jones, "Performing Post-Truth," 1.

48. German Lopez, "Why the country is having a big debate about empathy after Donald Trump's election" *Vox*, November 21, 2016, https://www.vox.com/policy-and-politics/2016/11/21/13642606/trump-voters-empathy-racism.

49. Lindsay B. Cummings, *Empathy as Dialogue in Theatre and Performance* (New York: Routledge, 2016), 6.

50. Cummings, *Empathy as Dialogue*, 193.

51. Duffy and Norris, *My Country*, 22.

52. O'Brien, "Divided by a Common Language," 13.

53. O'Brien, "Divided by a Common Language," 13.

54. Tom Nicholas, "*My Country.*"

55. Tony Fisher, "Introduction: Performance and the Tragic Politics of the *Agōn*," in *Performing Antagonism: Theatre, Performance & Radical Democracy*, ed. Tony Fisher and Eve Katsouraki (London: Palgrave Macmillan, 2017), 19.

56. Eve Katsouraki, "Epilogue: The 'Trojan Horse'—Or, from Antagonism to the Politics of Resilience" in *Performing Antagonism: Theatre, Performance & Radical Democracy*, ed. Tony Fisher and Eve Katsouraki (London: Palgrave Macmillan, 2017), 291.

57. Dean, *Democracy*, 94.

58. Tomlin, *Political Dramaturgies*, 129. Tomlin engages with this tension by weighing Jacques Rancière's notion of the emancipated spectator against the post-Marxist work of Chantal Mouffe in pursuit of radical democracy. Tomlin's provocative argument maintains that empathy remains a vital remedy for ironic neoliberal affects in ways that I admire, but that also seem beyond the scope of many of the more accessible entries into the form of verbatim theater.

59. Tomlin, *Political Dramaturgies*, 129.

60. Tomlin, *Political Dramaturgies*, 130.

61. Tomlin, *Political Dramaturgies*, 152.

62. Tomlin, *Political Dramaturgies*, 157.

63. Porte Parole, "About the Play: *The Assembly—Montreal*," https://porteparole.org/en/plays/the-assembly.

64. Alex Ivanovici, Annabel Soutar, and Brett Watson, "The Assembly—University of Maryland" (Production draft, November 2018). The company shared the script with me in January 2020, and also shared the rehearsal draft for the University of Maryland Assembly from November 2019. A full production of the University of Maryland Assembly has been delayed by the pandemic and, as of this writing, has not yet occurred.

65. Porte Parole, "The Assembly TRAILER 2020" January 2020, https://vimeo.

com/384561872. Moreover, in a separate interview, Ivanovici is quoted as saying, "The fact that public discourse itself seemed to be threatened made public discourse the subject of the show." Kate McKenna, "Think your family dinner is tense? New Montreal plays based on strangers debating politics over supper," *CBC News*, November 7, 2018, https://www.cbc.ca/news/canada/montreal/think-your-family-dinner-is-tense-new-montreal-plays-based-on-strangers-debating-politics-over-supper-1.4896469.

66. Ivanovici, Soutar, and Watson, "The Assembly—Montreal," 17.

67. Ivanovici, Soutar, and Watson, "The Assembly—Montreal," 35–36.

68. Ivanovici, Soutar, and Watson, "The Assembly—Montreal," 45.

69. Ivanovici, Soutar, and Watson, "The Assembly—Montreal," 47.

70. Ivanovici, Soutar, and Watson, "The Assembly—Montreal," 46.

71. Ivanovici, Soutar, and Watson, "The Assembly—Montreal," 51.

72. A number of sources might be located to illustrate the objection to hiding behind standards of civil discourse, including an oft-cited white paper on white supremacy culture, which has since been expanded to a more comprehensive web resource. Tema Okun, "White Supremacy Culture," *White Supremacy Culture*, https://www.whitesupremacyculture.info/uploads/4/3/5/7/43579015/characteristics_of_white_supremacy_culture-_original.jpg. More pithy is the (sometimes misattributed) Tweet by activist Robert Jones Jr., under the moniker Son of Baldwin. Robert Jones Jr., "We can disagree and still love each other unless your disagreement is rooted in my oppression and denial of my humanity and right to exist." @SonofBaldwin, August 18, 2015, 8:19 am, https://twitter.com/SonofBaldwin/status/633644373423562753.

73. Ivanovici, Soutar, and Watson, "The Assembly—Montreal," 46.

74. Ivanovici, Soutar, and Watson, "The Assembly—Montreal," 86.

75. Ivanovici, Soutar, and Watson, "The Assembly—Montreal," 87.

76. Ivanovici, Soutar, and Watson, "The Assembly—Montreal," 90–91 (emphasis original).

77. Tomlin, *Political Dramaturgies*, 17.

78. Tomlin, *Political Dramaturgies*, 17.

79. Ivanovici, Soutar, and Watson, "The Assembly—Montreal," 72.

80. J. Kelly Nestruck, "Review: The Assembly aims to illuminate, but only simulates today's divisive politics," *Globe and Mail*, October 31, 2018, https://www.theglobeandmail.com/arts/theatre-and-performance/reviews/article-review-the-assembly-aims-to-illuminate-but-only-simulates-todays/. Nestruck's review is pointed, closing, with "For *The Assembly* to be more than a platform for another charismatically un-PC alt-right figure to rile us up, some deconstruction was required. Instead, the show uses Valerie's full name, advertises her far-right organization and then it gives her an additional opportunity to spout off. Do its creators realize they've been used—or is *The Assembly*'s failure its point?" Other reviews are generally more positive about the perceived importance of the format including Aisling Murphy's

assertion that the performance should be considered "necessary viewing." Aisling Murphy, "Review of Porte Parole's *The Assembly—Montreal*," *The Theatre Times*, 30 March 2020, https://thetheatretimes.com/review-of-porte-paroles-the-assembly-montreal/.

81. Ivanovici, Soutar, and Watson, "The Assembly—University of Maryland," 101.

82. Ivanovici, Soutar, and Watson, "The Assembly—University of Maryland," 101.

83. Rich Lord, "How Robert Bowers Went from Conservative to White Nationalist," *Pittsburgh Post-Gazette*, November 10, 2018, https://www.post-gazette.com/news/crime-courts/2018/11/10/Robert-Bowers-extremism-Tree-of-Life-massacre-shooting-pittsburgh-Gab-Warroom/stories/201811080165.

84. Tomlin, *Political Dramaturgies*, 155–56.

85. Anna Deavere Smith, *Notes from the Field*. Aired Feburary 28, 2018 on HBO.

86. Anna Deavere Smith, "Toward Empathetic Imagination and Action," *Anna Deavere Smith*. Last accessed July 28, 2021, https://www.annadeaveresmith.org/category/notes-from-the-field/.

87. Torsten Ove, "Jewish congregation in Tree of Life massacre asks Attorney General Merrick Garland to forgo Bowers death penalty," *Pittsburgh Post-Gazette*, June 25, 2021, https://www.post-gazette.com/news/crime-courts/2021/06/25/Jewish-Tree-of-Life-synagogue-pittsburgh-mass-shooting-dor-hadash-letter-death-penalty-life-Attorney-General-Merrick-Garland-robert-bowers/stories/202106250104.

88. Ivanovici, Soutar, and Watson, "The Assembly—Montreal," 46.

CODA

1. Anna Deavere Smith, "The Last of the Nice Negro Girls," *The Atlantic*, March 2021, posted online February 9, 2021, https://www.theatlantic.com/magazine/archive/2021/03/the-last-of-the-nice-negro-girls/617786/.

2. Fredric Jameson, *The Political Unconscious: Narrative as a Socially Symbolic Act* (Ithaca, NY: Cornell University Press, 1981); Walter Benjamin, "Theses on the Philosophy of History," *Illuminations*, ed. Hannah Arendt (New York: Schocken Books, 1969), 253–64.

3. New verbatim work continues apace, even as the pandemic changed its modalities. For example, Jessica Blank and Erik Jensen's *Coal Country* ran at the Public Theater for 25 performances before the shuttering of the theaters in March 2020, at which point the duo immediately began work on the timely *The Line*, based on interviews with frontline medical workers in New York. That piece was produced by the Public and ran digitally from July 8 to September 1, 2020: about as present-focused as verbatim theater is ever going to get.

4. Svetlana Boym, *The Future of Nostalgia* (New York: Basic Books, 2001), xiii-xiv.

5. Adam Muller, "Notes toward a Theory of Nostalgia: Childhood and the Evocation of the past in Two European 'Heritage' Films," *New Literary History* 37, no. 4 (2006): 739, accessed August 4, 2021, http://www.jstor.org/stable/20057976.

6. Heidi Schlipphacke, "Postmodernism and the Place of Nostalgia in Ingeborg Bachmann's 'Franza' Fragment," *The German Quarterly* 79, no. 1 (2006): 71, accessed August 14, 2021, http://www.jstor.org/stable/27675885.

7. Benhabib, "The Embattled Public Sphere," 1.

8. Fredric Jameson, *Postmodernism; or, The Cultural Logic of Late Capitalism* (Durham, NC: Duke University Press, 1991), 19.

9. Linda Hutcheon and Mario J. Valdés, "Irony, Nostalgia, and the Postmodern: A Dialogue," *Poligrafías* 3 (1998–2000), 18, accessed August 14, 2021, http://revistas.unam.mx/index.php/poligrafias/article/viewFile/31312/28976.

10. Hutcheon and Valdés, "Irony, Nostalgia, and the Postmodern," 22.

11. Boym, *The Future of Nostalgia*, xv-xvi.

12. Boym, *The Future of Nostalgia*, 351.

13. Ben Brantley, "Review: Reflections that Sear in a Newly Reborn 'Fires in the Mirror,'" *New York Times*, November 11, 2019, https://www.nytimes.com/2019/11/11/theater/fires-in-the-mirror-signature.html.

14. Ben Brantley, "Review."

15. Ben Brantley, "Review," (emphasis added).

16. Vinson Cunningham, "The Urgency of Anna Deavere Smith's 'Twilight: Los Angeles,'" *The New Yorker*, August 24, 2020, https://www.newyorker.com/magazine/2020/08/24/-the-urgency-of-anna-deavere-smiths-twilight-los-angeles.

17. Vinson Cunningham, "The Urgency of Anna Deavere Smith's 'Twilight: Los Angeles.'"

18. Robert Eaglestone, "Cruel Nostalgia and the Memory of the Second World War," in *Brexit and Literature: Critical and Cultural Responses*, ed. Robert Eaglestone (Milton: Taylor & Francis Group, 2018), 92–104.

19. Diana Taylor, *The Archive and the Repertoire: Performing Cultural Memory in the Americas* (Durham: Duke University Press, 2003).

20. Rebecca Schneider, "That the Past May Yet Have Another Future: Gesture in the Times of Hands Up," *Theatre Journal* 70, no. 3 (2018): 306, https://doi.org/10.1353/tj.2018.0056.

21. Moisés Kaufman and the Members of the Tectonic Theater Project, *The Laramie Project and The Laramie Project: Ten Years Later* (New York: Vintage, 2014), 165.

22. Boym, *The Future of Nostalgia*, xiv.

23. Boym, *The Future of Nostalgia*, xv.

24. Kaufman, *The Laramie Project and The Laramie Project: Ten Years Later*, 181.

25. Kaufman, *The Laramie Project and The Laramie Project: Ten Years Later*, 172.

26. Kaufman, *The Laramie Project and The Laramie Project: Ten Years Later*, 187.

27. Kaufman, *The Laramie Project and The Laramie Project: Ten Years Later*, 105.

28. See, for example, Elizabeth Maupin, "Laramie isn't so Far from Grover's Corners," *Orlando Sentinel*, February 14, 2002, accessed August 14, 2021, https://www.orlandosentinel.com/news/os-xpm-2002-02-14-0202130437-story.html.

29. "State Scorecards," *Human Rights Campaign*, accessed August 14, 2021, https://www.hrc.org/resources/state-scorecards/p6.

30. *Twilight: Los Angeles, 1992*, written by Anna Deavere Smith, dir. Taibi Magar, Signature Theatre, New York City, November 6, 2021.

31. Jesse Green, "Review: Embodying Justice in 'Twilight: Los Angeles: 1992," *New York Times*, November 1, 2021, https://www.nytimes.com/2021/11/01/theater/twilight-los-angeles-1992-rodney-king.html.

32. Green, "Embodying Justice."

33. Green, "Embodying Justice."

34. Duffy and Norris, *My Country*, 58.

Bibliography

Ahmed, Sara. *The Cultural Politics of Emotion.* New York: Routledge, 2004.

Aikman, Lisa. "Dramaturging Research, Shaping Encounters: Working Methods and Dramaturgical Structures in Contemporary Canadian Documentary Theatre." PhD diss., University of Toronto, 2019.

Althusser, Louis. "Ideology and Ideological State Apparatuses." In *Lenin and Philosophy and Other Essays.* New York: Monthly Review Press, 1971.

Arjomand, Minou. "Performing Catastrophe: Erwin Piscator's Documentary Theatre." *Modern Drama* 59, no. 1 (2016): 49. https://www.muse.jhu.edu/article/611632.

Arjomand, Minou. *Staged: Show Trials, Political Theater, and the Aesthetics of Judgment.* New York: Columbia University Press, 2018.

Balme, Christopher. *The Theatrical Public Sphere.* Cambridge: Cambridge University Press, 2014.

Benhabib, Seyla. "The Embattled Public Sphere: Hannah Arendt, Juergen Habermas and Beyond." *Theoria: A Journal of Social and Political Theory,* no. 90 (1997): 15. Accessed August 9, 2021. http://www.jstor.org/stable/41802076.

Benhabib, Seyla. *Difference and Democracy.* Princeton, NJ: Princeton University Press, 1996.

Benjamin, Walter. "Theses on the Philosophy of History." *Illuminations.* Edited by Hannah Arendt. New York: Schocken Books, 1969.

Berlant, Lauren. *The Female Complaint: The Unfinished Business of Sentimentality on American Culture.* Durham, NC: Duke University Press, 2008.

Berlant, Lauren. *Cruel Optimism.* Durham, NC: Duke University Press, 2011.

Bernstein, Robin. "Rodney King, Shifting Modes of Vision, and Anna Deavere Smith's *Twilight: Los Angeles, 1992.*" *Journal of Dramatic Theory and Criticism* 14, no. 2 (Spring 2000): 130.

Billington, Michael. "*My Country: A Work in Progress* review—Carol Ann Duffy tackles Brexit." *Guardian,* March 12, 2017. https://www.theguardian.com/stage/2017/mar/12/my-country-a-work-in-progress-review-carol-ann-duffy-visits-brexit.

Black, Debra. "Dove anti-ageism campaign hits stage." *Thestar.com,* 9 May 2008. Web. 9Mar. 2011. Quoted in Moll, "Judith Thompson's *Body and Soul.*"

Black, Laura W. "Deliberation, Storytelling, and Dialogic Moments." *Communication Theory* 18, no. 1(2008): 93–116. https://doi.org/10.1111/j.1468–2885.2007.00315.x.

Blair, Rhonda. "Cognitive Neuroscience and Acting: Imagination, Conceptual Blending, and Empathy." *TDR/The Drama Review* 53, no. 4 (204) (2009): 102. https://doi.org/10.1162/dram.2009.53.4.93.

Blair, Rhonda. *The Actor, Image, and Action: Acting and Cognitive Neuroscience.* London: Routledge, 2008.

Blankenship, Lisa. *Changing the Subject: A Theory of Rhetorical Empathy.* Louisville, Colo.: University Press of Colorado, 2019.

Bowditch, Rachel. *On the Edge of Utopia: Performance and Ritual at Burning Man.* London, Seagull Books, 2010.

Boym, Svetlana. *The Future of Nostalgia.* New York: Basic Books, 2001.

Brantley, Ben. "Review: Reflections that Sear in a Newly Reborn 'Fires in the Mirror.'" *New York Times,* November 11, 2019. https://www.nytimes.com/2019/11/11/theater/fires-in-the-mirror-signature.html.

Brantley, Ben. "Theater Review: A Brutal Act Alters a Town." *New York Times,* May 19, 2000. https://www.nytimes.com/2000/05/19/movies/theater-review-a-brutal-act-alters-a-town.html.

Breithaupt, Fritz. *The Dark Sides of Empathy.* Translated by Andrew B. B. Hamilton. Ithaca, NY: Cornell University Press, 2019.

Brown, Wendy. *Undoing the Demos: Neoliberalism's Stealth Revolution.* New York: Zone Books, 2015.

Canby, Vincent. "When Communists clashed with Nazis and the Klan." Review of *Greensboro: A Requiem. New York Times,* February 12, 1996, C11. https://www.nytimes.com/1996/02/12/theater/theater-review-when-communists-clashed-with-nazis-and-the-klan.html.

Casson, John W. "Living Newspaper: Theatre and Therapy." *TDR: The Drama Review* 44, no. 2 (2000): 107–22. https://www.muse.jhu.edu/article/33003.

Chambers, Simone. "Rhetoric and the Public Sphere: Has Deliberative Democracy Abandoned Mass Democracy?" *Political Theory* 37, no. 3 (June 2009): 324.

Chong, Ping, and Alisa Solomon. *Undesirable Elements: Real People, Real Lives, Real Theater.* New York: Theatre Communications Group, 2012.

Clapp, Susannah. "*My Country: A Work in Progress* review—A laudable but limp look at Brexit Britain." *Guardian,* March 19, 2017. https://www.theguardian.com/stage/2017/mar/19/my-country-work-in-progress-dorfman-observer-review.

Claycomb, Ryan. "Voices from No-Where: Space, Place and the Utopian Impulse of Oral History Performance." (Plenary presentation at Oral History and Performance Conference for Oral History of the Mid-Atlantic Region at Columbia University, New York, NY, March 13–15, 2008.)

Claycomb, Ryan. "(Ch)oral History: Docudrama, the Communal Subject, and Progressive Form." *Journal of Dramatic Theory and Criticism* 17:2 (Spring 2003): 95–121.

Claycomb, Ryan. "Exceptional Embodiment in Anna Deavere Smith's *Let Me Down*

Easy." In *Critical Perspectives on Contemporary Playwriting by Women: The Early Twenty-First Century*, ed. Penny Farfan and Lesley Ferris, 168. Ann Arbor: University of Michigan Press, 2021.

Claycomb, Ryan. "Playing at Lives: Life Writing and Contemporary Feminist Drama." Doctoral diss., University of Maryland, College Park, 2003.

Claycomb, Ryan. Review of *Guantanamo: 'Honor Bound to Defend Freedom.' Theatre Journal* 58, no. 4 (2006): 703-705. https://doi.org/10.1353/tj.2007.0006.

Claycomb, Ryan. "Staging the Inscrutable Terrorist: Brittain and Slovo's *Guantanamo: 'Honor Bound to Defend Freedom.'*" *Politics and Culture* (2007):1. http://aspen.conncoll.edu/politicsandculture/.

Claycomb, Ryan. "The Document and the Account: The Dramaturgy of Truth Claims in Oral History and Documentary Performances." (Paper presented for "The Post-Truth Historian" Working Group at the American Society for Theatre Research 2013 Conference in Dallas TX, November 7–10, 2013.)

Claycomb, Ryan. "Voices of the Other: Documentary and Oral History Performance in Post-9/11 British Theatre." In *Political and Protest Theatre after 9/11: Patriotic Dissent*, ed. Jenny Spencer, 93–107. New York: Routledge, 2011.

Crompton, Sarah. "Review: *My Country: A Work in Progress*," *WhatsOnStage*, March 10, 2017. https://www.whatsonstage.com/london-theatre/reviews/my-country-a-work-in-progress-dorfman-national_43092.html.

Cummings, Lindsay B. *Empathy as Dialogue in Theatre and Performance*. New York: Routledge, 2016.

Cunningham, Vinson. "The Urgency of Anna Deavere Smith's 'Twilight: Los Angeles.'" *New Yorker*, August 24, 2020. https://www.newyorker.com/magazine/2020/08/24/-the-urgency-of-anna-deavere-smiths-twilight-los-angeles.

Dahlberg, Lincoln. "The Habermasian Public Sphere: Taking Difference Seriously?" *Theory and Society* 34 (2005): 111–36.

Davies, Paul T. "REVIEW: *My Country—A Work in Progress.*" *BritishTheatre.com*, March 11, 2017. https://britishtheatre.com/review-my-country-a-work-in-progress-national-theatre/.

Dawson, Gary Fisher. *Documentary Theatre in the United States.* Westport, Conn.: Greenwood Press, 1999.

de Certeau, Michel. *The Practice of Everyday Life.* London: University of California Press, 1984.

Dean, Jodi. *Democracy and Other Neoliberal Fantasies: Communicative Capitalism and Left Politics.* Durham, NC: Duke University Press, 2009.

Dolan, Jill. *Utopia in Performance: Finding Hope at the Theater.* Ann Arbor: University of Michigan Press, 2005.

Duffy, Carol Ann, and Rufus Norris. *My Country; A Work in Progress.* London: Faber & Faber, 2019.

Duggan, Lisa. *The Twilight of Equality: Neoliberal Cultural Politics and the Attack on Democracy.* Boston: Beacon Press, 2003.

DuPlessis, Rachel Blau. *Writing Beyond the Ending: Narrative Strategies of Twentieth-Century Women Writers.* Bloomington, Ind.: Indiana University Press, 1985.

Eaglestone, Robert. "Cruel Nostalgia and the Memory of the Second World War." In *Brexit and Literature: Critical and Cultural Responses*, ed. Robert Eaglestone, 92–104. Milton: Taylor & Francis Group, 2018.

Edgar, David. "Doc and dram: Why has this decade seen the rise of a vibrant theatre of reportage?" *Guardian* (London), September 27, 2008, 18. https://www.theguardian.com/stage/2008/sep/27/theatre.davidedgar.

Ellis, Atiba R. "The Meme of Voter Fraud." *Catholic University Law Review* 63 (2014): 879. https://scholarship.law.edu/lawreview/vol63/iss4/2.

Ensler, Eve. *The Vagina Monologues.* New York: Villard, 1998.

Eres, Robert, and Pascal Molenberghs, "The influence of group membership on the neural correlates involved in empathy." *Frontiers in Human Neuroscience* Volume 7, Article 176 (May 2013): 1–5. https://doi.org/10.3389/fnhum.2013.00176.

Favorini, Attilio. *Voicings: Ten Plays from the Documentary Theater.* Hopewell, NJ: Ecco Press, 1995.

Felski, Rita. *The Limits of Critique.* Chicago: University of Chicago Press, 2015.

Filewod, Alan. *Collective Encounters: Documentary Theatre in English Canada.* Toronto: University of Toronto Press, 1987.

Fisher, Tony. "Introduction: Performance and the Tragic Politics of the *Agōn.*" In *Performing Antagonism: Theatre, Performance & Radical Democracy*, ed. Tony Fisher and Eve Katsouraki, 19. London: Palgrave Macmillan, 2017.

Fleckenstein, Kristie S. "Once Again with Feeling: Empathy in Deliberative Discourse." *JAC* 27, no. 3/4 (2007): 701–16. www.jstor.org/stable/20866807.

Flynn, Molly. *Witness onstage: Documentary theatre in twenty-first-century Russia.* Manchester, UK: Manchester University Press, 2020.

Forsyth, Alison, and Chris Megson. *Get Real: Documentary Theatre Past and Present.* New York: Palgrave Macmillan, 2009.

Foucault, Michel. *History of Sexuality, vol. 1: An Introduction.* New York: Vintage, 1990.

Gallagher-Ross, Jacob. *Theaters of the Everyday: Aesthetic Democracy on the American Stage.* Evanston, Ill.: Northwestern University Press, 2018.

Garde, Ulrike, and Meg Mumford. "Postdramatic Reality Theatre and Productive Insecurity: Destabilising Encounters with the Unfamiliar in Theatre from Sydney and Berlin." In *Postdramatic Theatre and the Political*, ed. Karen Jürs-Munby, Jerome Carroll, and Steve Giles, 147–64. London: Bloomsbury, 2013.

Garner, Stanton B., Jr. *Bodied Spaces: Phenomenology and Performance in Contemporary Drama.* Ithaca: Cornell University Press, 1994.

Geuss, Raymond. "A Republic of Discussion: Habermas at Ninety." *The Point*, June 18, 2019. https://thepointmag.com/politics/a-republic-of-discussion-habermas-at-ninety/.

Geuss, Raymond. *The Idea of a Critical Theory: Habermas and the Frankfurt School.* Cambridge, UK: Cambridge University Press, 1981.

Green, Jesse. "Review: Embodying Justice in 'Twilight: Los Angeles, 1992.'" *New York Times*, November 1, 2021. https://www.nytimes.com/2021/11/01/theater/twilight-los-angeles-1992-rodney-king.html.

Gutmann, Amy, and Dennis F. Thompson. *Why Deliberative Democracy?* Princeton: NJ: Princeton University Press, 2004.

Habermas, Jürgen. *The Structural Transformation of the Public Sphere*. Translated by Thomas Burger and Frederick Lawrence. Boston: MIT Press, 1989.

Habermas, Jürgen. *The Theory of Communicative Action: Reason and the Rationalization of Society, volume 1*. Translated by Thomas McCarthy. Boston: Beacon Press, 1989.

Hare, David. *Stuff Happens*. London: Faber and Faber, 2005.

Harvey, David. *A Brief History of Neoliberalism*. Oxford: Oxford UP, 2005.

Hutcheon, Linda, and Mario J. Valdés. "Irony, Nostalgia, and the Postmodern: A Dialogue." *Poligrafías* 3 (1998–2000): 18. Accessed August 14, 2021. http://revistas.unam.mx/index.php/poligrafias/article/viewFile/31312/28976.

Isherwood, Charles. "Woman of 1,000 Faces Considers the Body." Review of *Let Me Down Easy*. *New York Times*, October 7, 2009. https://www.nytimes.com/2009/10/08/theater/reviews/08easy.html.

Ivanovici, Alex, Annabel Soutar, and Brett Watson. "The Assembly—Montreal" (Production draft, November 2018; Performance by Porte Parole Theatre). Accessed February 20, 2020. https://porteparole.org/en/plays/the-assembly/.

Ivanovici, Alex, Annabel Soutar, and Brett Watson. "The Assembly—University of Maryland" (Production Draft, November 2018).

Jameson, Fredric. *Postmodernism, or, The Cultural Logic of Late Capitalism*. Durham, NC: Duke University Press, 1991.

Jameson, Fredric. *The Political Unconscious: Narrative as a Socially Symbolic Act*. Ithaca, NY: Cornell University Press, 1981.

Jay, Gregory S. "Other People's Holocausts: Trauma, Empathy, and Justice in Anna Deavere Smith's *Fires in the Mirror*." *Contemporary Literature* 48, no. 1 (2007): 130. https://doi.org/10.1353/cli.2007.0024.

Jones, Robert, Jr. "We can disagree and still love each other unless your disagreement is rooted in my oppression and denial of my humanity and right to exist." @SonofBaldwin August 18, 2015, 8:19 am. https://twitter.com/SonofBaldwin/status/633644373423562753.

Jones, Matt. "Performing Post-Truth: An Interview with Director Ashlie Corcoran." *Theatre Journal* 72, no. 1 (2020): E-1–E-6. https://doi.org/10.1353/tj.2020.0000.

Katsouraki, Eve. "Epilogue: The 'Trojan Horse'—Or, from Antagonism to the Politics of Resilience." In *Performing Antagonism: Theatre, Performance & Radical Democracy*, ed. Tony Fisher and Eve Katsouraki, 291. London: Palgrave Macmillan, 2017.

Kaufman, Moisés, and the members of the Tectonic Theater Project. *The Laramie Project*. DVD. Directed by Moisés Kaufman. HBO Home Video, 2002.

Kaufman, Moisés, and the Members of the Tectonic Theater Project. *The Laramie Project and The Laramie Project: Ten Years Later*. New York: Vintage, 2014.

Keen, Suzanne. *Empathy and the Novel.* Oxford: Oxford University Press, 2010.

Kershaw, Baz. *The Radical in Performance: Between Brecht and Baudrillard.* London: Routledge, 1999.

Lanzoni, Susan. *Empathy: A History.* New Haven, Conn.: Yale University Press, 2018.

Leong, Nancy. "Racial Capitalism." *Harvard Law Review* 126, no. 8 (2013): 2153–226.

"LGBTQ Memorials: Matthew Shepard Memorial, Laramie, WY." *Finding Our Place: LGBTQ Memorials in America.* National Park Service, 20 February 2018. https://www.nps.gov/articles/lgbtq-memorials-matthew-shepard-memorial-laramie-wy.htm.

Lopez, German. "Why the country is having a big debate about empathy after Donald Trump's election." *Vox*, November 21, 2016. https://www.vox.com/policy-and-politics/2016/11/21/13642606/trump-voters-empathy-racism.

Lord, Rich. "How Robert Bowers Went from Conservative to White Nationalist." *Pittsburgh Post-Gazette*, November 10, 2018. https://www.post-gazette.com/news/crime-courts/2018/11/10/Robert-Bowers-extremism-Tree-of-Life-massacre-shooting-pittsburgh-Gab-Warroom/stories/201811080165.

Mann, Emily. "Greensboro: A Requiem." In *Testimonies: Four Plays, 247–330.* New York: Theatre Communications Group, 1997.

Martin, Carol. *Dramaturgy of the Real on the World Stage.* United Kingdom: Palgrave Macmillan UK, 2010).

Martin, Carol. Guest Editor, Special Issue on Documentary Theatre. *TDR: The Drama Review* 50, no. 3 (2006). https://www.muse.jhu.edu/article/201932.

Martin, Carol. *Theatre of the Real.* New York: Palgrave Macmillan, 2013.

Mason, Gregory. "Documentary Drama from the Revue to the Tribunal." *Modern Drama* 20, no. 3 (Fall 1977): 275. https://doi.org/10.1353/mdr.1977.0047.

Mathog, Nuria. "LGBT youth reflect on experiences in community." *The Laramie Boomerang*, 22 October 2015. https://www.laramieboomerang.com/news/local_news/lgbt-youth-reflect-on-experiences-in-community/article_46702524-6eff-11e5-ab6d-7329bf86b8af.html.

"Matthew Shepard Murder Site." *Finding Brokeback.* Accessed November 12, 2020. http://www.findingbrokeback.com/Entering_Wyoming/Shepard_Murder.html.

Maupin, Elizabeth. "Laramie isn't so Far from Grover's Corners." *Orlando Sentinel*, February 14, 2002. Accessed August 14, 2021. https://www.orlandosentinel.com/news/os-xpm-2002-02-14-0202130437-story.html.

McCorgray, Daisy. "My Country: This Brexit play actually listened to people in the UK." *The New European*, 3 March 2017. https://www.theneweuropean.co.uk/brexit-news/my-country-this-brexit-play-actually-listened-to-people-in-16920/.

McKenna, Kate. "Think your family dinner is tense? New Montreal plays based on strangers debating politics over supper." *CBC News*, November 7, 2018. https://www.cbc.ca/news/canada/montreal/think-your-family-dinner-is-tense-new-montreal-plays-based-on-strangers-debating-politics-over-supper-1.4896469.

McKinley, Jesse. "Bringing the High Drama of Real Life to the Stage." *New York Times*, Feb 27, 2000. https://www.nytimes.com/2000/02/27/theater/spring-theater-visions-america-bringing-high-drama-real-life-stage.html.

Misitzis, Lina, Hanna Rosin, and Alix Spiegel. "The End of Empathy." *Invisibilia*. Season 5, episode 6. April 11, 2019. National Public Radio. https://www.npr.org/transcripts/712276022.

Moll, Sorouja. "Judith Thompson's *Body and Soul*: Tactics of Theatre in the Corporate Strategy." *Canadian Theatre Review* 148 (2011): 48. https://doi.org/10.1353/ctr.2011.0076.

Moore, John. "The Enduring Legacy of 'Laramie,' Two Decades Later." *American Theatre*, February 26, 2020. https://www.americantheatre.org/2020/02/26/the-enduring-legacy-of-laramie-two-decades-later/.

Muller, Adam. "Notes toward a Theory of Nostalgia: Childhood and the Evocation of the Past in Two European 'Heritage' Films." *New Literary History* 37, no. 4 (2006): 739. Accessed August 4, 2021. http://www.jstor.org/stable/20057976.

Muñoz, José Esteban. *Cruising Utopia: The Then and There of Queer Futurity*. New York: New York University Press, 2009.

Murphy, Aisling. "Review of Porte Parole's *The Assembly—Montreal*." *The Theatre Times*, 30 March 2020. https://thetheatretimes.com/review-of-porte-paroles-the-assembly-montreal/.

Nadler, Paul. "Liberty Censored: Black Living Newspapers of the Federal Theatre Project." *African American Review* 29, no. 4 (1995): 618–19. Accessed February 13, 2020. https://doi.org/10.2307/3042154.

National Endowment for the Humanities. "Anna Deavere Smith: Jefferson Lecture, 2015." *NEH.gov*. https://www.neh.gov/about/awards/jefferson-lecture/anna-deavere-smith-biography.

Nestruck, J. Kelly. "Review: The Assembly aims to illuminate, but only simulates today's divisive politics." *Globe and Mail*, October 31, 2018. https://www.theglobeandmail.com/arts/theatre-and-performance/reviews/article-review-the-assembly-aims-to-illuminate-but-only-simulates-todays/.

Nicholas, Tom. "*My Country* by Carol Ann Duffy and Rufus Norris at National Theatre London | Performance Analysis." *Tom Nicholas: Theory, Politics, Culture*. March 14, 2017. Recording currently listed as private and shared privately by the author. Last accessed July 28, 2021. https://www.youtube.com/channel/UCxt2r-57cLastdmrReiQJkEg.

Norton-Taylor, Richard, et al. *The Tricycle: Collected Tribunal Plays: 1994–2012*. London: Oberon Books, 2015.

O'Brien, Shauna. "'Divided by a Common Language': The Use of Verbatim in Carol Ann Duffy and Rufus Norris' *My Country; A Work in Progress*." *Humanities* 8, no. 1 (2019): 58. https://doi.org/10.3390/h80100582.

O'Connor, Jacqueline. *Documentary Trial Plays in Contemporary American Theater*. Carbondale, Ill.: Southern Illinois University Press, 2013.

O'Thomas, Mark. "*My Country*: A Play about Brexit that Tries to Break the Bubble but Disappoints." *The Conversation*, March 21, 2017. https://theconversation.com/my-country-a-play-about-brexit-that-tries-to-break-the-bubble-but-disappoints-74388.

Okun, Tema. "White Supremacy Culture." *White Supremacy Culture*. https://www.whitesupremacyculture.info/uploads/4/3/5/7/43579015/characteristics_of_white_supremacy_culture-_original.jpg.

Ove, Torsten. "Jewish congregation in Tree of Life massacre asks Attorney General Merrick Garland to forgo Bowers death penalty." *Pittsburgh Post-Gazette*, June 25, 2021. https://www.post-gazette.com/news/crime-courts/2021/06/25/Jewish-Tree-of-Life-synagogue-pittsburgh-mass-shooting-dor-hadash-letter-death-penalty-life-Attorney-General-Merrick-Garland-robert-bowers/stories/202106250104.

Pedwell, Carolyn C. *Affective Relations: The Transnational Politics of Empathy*. London: Palgrave Macmillan UK, 2014.

Pollock, Della. "Introduction: Remembering." In *Remembering: Oral History Performance*, 2. New York: Palgrave Macmillan, 2005.

Porte Parole. "The Assembly TRAILER 2020." January 2020. https://vimeo.com/384561872.

Porte Parole. "About the Play: *The Assembly—Montreal*." https://porteparole.org/en/plays/the-assembly.

Reinelt, Janelle. "The Promise of Documentary." In *Get Real: Documentary Theatre Past and Present*, ed. Alison Forsyth and Chris Megson, 7. Basingstoke: Palgrave, 2009.

Reinelt, Janelle. "Performing Race: Anna Deavere Smith's *Fires in the Mirror*." *Modern Drama* 39, no. 4 (1996): 609–17. https://doi.org/10.1353/mdr.1996.0090.

Reynolds, Dee, and Matthew Reason. *Kinesthetic Empathy in Creative and Cultural Practice*. Bristol, UK: Intellect Books, 2012.

Ritivoi, Andreea Deciu. "Reading Stories, Reading (Others') Lives: Empathy, Intersubjectivity, and Narrative Understanding." *Storyworlds: A Journal of Narrative Studies* 8, no. 1 (2016): 51–75. Accessed May 24, 2021. https://doi.org/10.5250/storyworlds.8.1.0051.

Ruiz, Didier. *TRANS (MÉS ENLLÀ)* (performance at Festival D'Avignon, at Gymnase du lycée Mistral, Avignon, France, in July 2018). Accessed February 20, 2020. https://www.festival-avignon.com/en/shows/2018/trans-mes-enlla/.

Ryfe, David M. "Narrative and Deliberation in Small Group Forums." *Journal of Applied Communication Research* 34, no. 1 (2006): 72–93. https://doi.org/10.1080/00909880500420226.

Savran, David. "Ambivalence, Utopia, and a Queer Sort of Materialism: How Angels in America Reconstructs the Nation." *Theatre Journal* 47 (1995): 226.

Schlipphacke, Heidi. "Postmodernism and the Place of Nostalgia in Ingeborg Bachmann's 'Franza' Fragment." *The German Quarterly* 79, no. 1 (2006): 71. Accessed August 14, 2021. http://www.jstor.org/stable/27675885.

Schneider, Rebecca. "That the Past May Yet Have Another Future: Gesture in the Times of Hands Up." *Theatre Journal* 70, no. 3 (2018): 306. https://doi.org/10.1353/tj.2018.0056.

Shaw, Helen. "The Decade in Theater: Six Closing Thoughts" What Were the 2010s? *Vulture*, December 31, 2019. https://www.vulture.com/2019/12/the-2010s-in-theater-spidey-hamilton-gatz-and-much-more.html/.

Sierz, Aleks. Review of *My Country; A Work in Progress*, National Theatre. *Aleks Sierz*, March 10, 2017. https://www.sierz.co.uk/reviews/my-country-a-work-in-progress-national-theatre/. Originally published in *The Arts Desk*, https://www.theartsdesk.com/.

Smith, Anna Deavere. "The Last of the Nice Negro Girls." *The Atlantic*, March 2021, posted online February 9, 2021. https://www.theatlantic.com/magazine/archive/2021/03/the-last-of-the-nice-negro-girls/617786/.

Smith, Anna Deavere. "Toward Empathetic Imagination and Action." *Anna Deavere Smith*. Last accessed July 28, 2021. https://www.annadeaveresmith.org/category/notes-from-the-field/.

Smith, Anna Deavere. *Fires in the Mirror*. New York: Anchor Books, 1993.

Smith, Anna Deavere. *Let Me Down Easy*. New York: Theatre Communications Group, 2018.

Smith, Anna Deavere. *Notes from the Field*. New York: Anchor Books, 2019.

Smith, Anna Deavere. *Notes from the Field*. Aired February 28, 2018 on HBO.

Smith, Anna Deavere. *Twilight: Los Angeles, 1992*. Performance at Ford's Theatre, Washington, DC, February 9, 1997.

Smith, Anna Deavere. *Twilight: Los Angeles, 1992*. New York: Anchor Books, 1994.

Smith, Anna Deavere. *Twilight: Los Angeles, 1992*. Directed by Marc Levin. Performed by Anna Deavere Smith (PBS Pictures, 2000). VHS.

Smith, Anna Deavere. *Twilight: Los Angeles, 1992*. Directed by Taibi Magar. Performance at Signature Theatre, New York City, November 6, 2021.

Snyder-Young, Dani. *Theatre of Good Intentions: Challenges and Hopes for Theatre and Social Change*. New York: Palgrave Macmillan, 2013.

Soans, Robin. *Talking to Terrorists*. London: Oberon Books, 2006.

"State Scorecards" Human Rights Campaign. Accessed August 14, 2021. https://www.hrc.org/resources/state-scorecards/p6.

States, Bert O. *Great Reckonings in Little Rooms: On the Phenomenology of Theater*. Berkeley: University of California Press, 1985.

Stephenson, Jenn. *Insecurity: Perils and Products of Theatres of the Real*. Toronto: University of Toronto Press, 2019.

Stewart, D-L. "Language of Appeasement." *Inside Higher Ed*, March 30, 2017. https://www.insidehighered.com/views/2017/03/30/colleges-need-language-shift-not-one-you-think-essay.

Stocker, Susan G. "Problems of Embodiment and Problematic Embodiment." *Hypatia* 16, no. 3 (Summer 2001): 30–55.

Stuart Fisher, Amanda. *Performing the testimonial: rethinking verbatim strategies.* Manchester, UK: Manchester University Press, 2020.

Swain, Elise. "It's Still Open: Will the Guantánamo Bay Prison Become a 2020 Issue?" *The Intercept*, March 3, 2019. https://theintercept.com/2019/03/03/Guantánamo-bay-carol-rosenberg-intercepted/.

Taylor, Diana. *The Archive and the Repertoire: Performing Cultural Memory in the Americas.* Durham: Duke University Press, 2003.

Theatrical Outfit. "*Our Town* and *The Laramie Project*." Accessed August 14, 2021. https://www.theatricaloutfit.org/shows/our-town-and-the-laramie-project/.

Tomlin, Liz. *Political Dramaturgies and Theatre Spectatorship: Provocations for Change.* London: Methuen Drama, 2019.

Welna, David. "Trump has Vowed to Fill Guantánamo with Some Bad Dudes—But Who?" *All Things Considered.* National Public Radio (November 14, 2016). https://www.npr.org/sections/parallels/2016/11/14/502007304/trump-has-vowed-to-fill-Guantánamo-with-some-bad-dudes-but-who.

Yachnin, Paul, and Bronwen Wilson, eds. *Making Publics in Early Modern Europe: people, things, and forms of knowledge.* New York: Routledge, 2010.

Yachnin, Paul, and Marlene Eberhart, eds. *Forms of Association: Making Publics in Early Modern Europe*, Massachusetts Studies in Early Modern Culture. Amherst: University of Massachusetts Press, 2015.

Yi-Fu Tuan. *Space and Place: The Perspective of Experience.* Minneapolis: University of Minnesota Press, 1977.

Young, Iris Marion. *Inclusion and Democracy.* Oxford: Oxford University Press, 2000.

Zatz, Sara. "Methodology: An Overview." In Ping Chong, *Undesirable Elements: Real People, Real Lives, Real Theater, 207.* New York: Theatre Communications Group, 2012.

Zhao, Guoping. "The Public and Its Problem: Dewey, Habermas, and Levinas." *Journal of Educational Controversy* 8, no. 1 (2014): 10.

Zilliacus, Clas. "Documentary Drama: Form and Content." *Comparative Drama* 6, no. 3 (Fall 1972): 224.

Index